W9-AUM-932

LOST
The Ultimate Unofficial Guide of ABC's Hit Series LOST

Season One

By Rebecca K. O'Connor & Jim Stewart

Equity Press

Please visit our website at www.lost-book.com

© 2006 Equity Press all rights reserved.

ISBN 1-933804-03-3

All rights reserved. No part of this publication may be reproduced, stored in a retrieval system, or transmitted in any form or by any means, electronic, mechanical, photocopying, recording or otherwise, without either the prior written permission of the publisher or a license permitting restricted copying in the United States or abroad.

The information in this book has been included for news and interpretation value only. The facts been verified with care but are not guaranteed for any particular purpose. The publisher does not offer any warranties or representations not does it accept any liabilities with respect to the information in this book.

Trademark notices

DISCLAIMER: This book is unofficial and unauthorized. It is not authorized, approved, licensed, or endorsed by ABC, Lost, it's producers, writers, distributors, publishers, or licensors. Any use of the trademarks and character names is strictly for the purpose of analysis and news reporting. All material related to the analysis is © ABC © JJ Abrams and © Damon Lindelof © LOST

Table of Contents

LOST Characters

Major Players
(In Alphabetical Order)

Boone Carlyle *(Ian Somerhalder):* Boone is the Chief Operating Officer of the family wedding business, but was in Australia to rescue Shannon from yet another bad relationship.

Charlie Pace *(Dominic Monaghan):* Charlie is a drug-addicted and aspiring "rock god". He was in Sydney trying to convince his brother to rejoin their band Drive Shaft in the hopes of making a comeback, but left for Los Angeles alone.

Claire Littleton *(Emilie De Ravin):* Claire is unwed and eight months pregnant on her way to give up her child to adoptive parents in Los Angeles. She was encouraged to take the trip by a psychic would have supposedly arranged the adoption.

Hugo "**Hurley**" Reyes *(Jorge Garcia):* Hurley won $156 million in the lottery and has no end of personal good luck, but for those around him, bad luck abounds. Believing himself cursed by the lottery numbers, he went to Australia to find answers.

Jack Shephard *(Matthew Fox)*: Jack is a spinal surgeon who was on the plan bringing his father's body back to Los Angeles. He emerges as the leader of the group, although initially with reluctance.

Jin – Soo Kwon *(Daniel Dae Kim):* Forced to work for Sun's father to win her hand, Jin has become a "yes man" to his powerful and brutal father-in-law. He was planning to run away with his wife and escape his influence once they made it to the United States.

10

Kate Austen *(Evangeline Lilly):* Kate is a fugitive who has been on the run for the last three years. The marshal that finally caught her was extraditing her back to the United States.

John **Locke** *(Terry O'Quinn):* Locke is a manager for a box company, but dreams of life-changing adventure. He went to Australia to join in a "walk-about," but was turned away because he was in a wheel chair. Miraculously after the crash, Locke found that he had regained the use of his limbs.

Michael Dawson *(Harold Perrineau):* Michael is a construction worker and artist who went to Sydney to retrieve his estranged but beloved son after the death of his son's mother.

"Sawyer" James Ford *(Josh Holloway):* A con man with a troubled past, Sawyer was in Australia trying to settle an old score.

Sayid Jarrah *(Naveen Andrews):* Sayid is a former Iraqi soldier who excels at fixing things and reluctantly in torture. He was on his way to Los Angeles to find a lost love.

Shannon Rutherford *(Maggie Grace):* Shannon's main occupation is socialite and troublemaker, but was in Australian engaged in a plan to dupe her step-brother out a large chunk of money.

Sun Kwon *(Yunjin Kim):* Trapped in a troubled marriage to a domineering man, Sun had given up on her husband being the man with whom she had fallen in love. She had planned to run away from the airport, but a kind gesture changed her mind.

Walt *(Malcolm David Kelly):* Walt is an intelligent boy with seemingly strange powers to make things happen. This unsettled his step-father who summoned his real father to take him back to the United States.

Minor Characters (with major influence)

Noor "Nadia" Abed-Jazeem: Sayid's old friend and love interest that ends his career in the Republican Guard.

Tom Brennan – Kate's childhood sweetheart whose death was a result of Kate running form the police.

Anthony Cooper – Locke's estranged father.

Frank Duckett – The man that Sawyer is duped into shooting.

Helen – John Locke's love interest.

Aaron Littleton – Claire's son born on the island.

Emily Annabel Locke – Locke's estranged mother who suddenly appeared in his life.

Richard Malkin- The psychic that tells Claire she must raise her own child for the better or there will be consequences.

Edward Mars – The Marshal who chased Kate for many years before he caught up to her, only to suffer a mortal wound in the plane crash.

Ray Mullin – The kind-hearted farmer that took Kate in only to later turn her in to the authorities.

Susan Lloyd-Porter- Michael's ex-lover and the mother of Walt.

Ethan Rom- A man who wasn't on the plane and likely is one of the others.

Randy- Locke's boss at the box company.

Rose – One of the 48 survivors that survived the initial crash. She is convinced that her husband Bernard who was at the back of the plane is still alive.

Danielle Rousseau – The French woman who was stranded on the island with her scientific expedition more than sixteen years ago.

Christian Shephard- Jack's estranged father.

Margo Shephard – Jack's mother.

Sarah Shephard – The woman that Jack saved in surgery that ultimately becomes his wife.

Lenny Sims – The man in the mental institution from whom Hurley learned the numbers.

Sam Toomey – The man who was with Lenny Sims when he first heard the numbers.

Martha Toomey – Sam Toomey's wife.

What's in a Name?

Writers never "accidentally" name characters. Here's some speculation on names.

Episode One – Pilot Part 1

Summary

Jack, the "leader" of the LOST survivors, wakes up in the jungle, injured and confused. Sounds of chaos reach him and he rises to run toward the plane wreck and the beach. For a moment he finds serene untouched white sands and ocean. Then he turns and runs, discovering complete chaos.

Jack hears someone screaming for help and takes a hard look around him. Jack finds the source of the calls for help, a man trapped and screaming under a tire with the metal still attached. Jack calls for assistance and several survivors help him lift the wreckage and pull the wounded man free. Jack rips open the man's pants and finds his leg is a mangled mess. Yet Jack doesn't wince, he simply jumps into action. As Jack uses his tie as a tourniquet, he hears another cry for help, Claire's.

Jack looks around and sees Locke is one of the men that helped. He yells to him over the noise to help move the man away from the dangerously spinning engine. Jack runs around the engine to Claire, who is obviously pregnant, but it's not time for the baby to be born. Jack is intent on helping Claire, but takes a look around him to see another needy patient. Boone is trying to do CPR on Rose unsuccessfully.

While Jack is busy, Locke and another man are helping the survivor with an injured leg to a safer place. Locke looks up to see a man running by the jet engine and he's way too close. Locke yells at him to get away, but when the man stops to try to figure out what Locke is telling him, he's sucked into the engine. The engine explodes and further chaos erupts.

Debris is raining all over what is already a minefield, but Jack is now focused on the woman who is obviously dying in Boone's care. Jack notices Hurley and yells for him to come help him. He instructs Hurley to move Claire away from the fumes and keep tabs on her contractions.

Jack rushes to Boone and takes over his attempts at CPR. Boone suggests that they should do one of those "hole things" where they stick a pen in her throat, Jack eagerly sends him to get a pen. It's only to get rid of him however, and Jack goes back to desperately trying to get the woman to breathe on her own. Suddenly Rose coughs and begins to breathe, but there's no time to revel in the miracle.

The sound of tortured metal signals that the wing suspended above Claire and Hurley is about to plummet to the ground and crush them both. Jack runs to them as fast as he can screaming. Together Jack and Hurley just barely get Claire out of the way as the wing falls and explodes, the remaining engine exploding along with it.

Jack finds some luggage, opening a suitcase that obviously belonged to a woman. Rifling through the suitcase Jack finds a cosmetic bag. When he opens it, he pulls out a sewing kit. With the sewing kit in hand Jack finds a secluded place by the beach. He has a large gash on his back that he can't quite reach and even trying to tend to it is painful. He looks around as if trying to decide what to do and Kate appears dazed and holding on to her right wrist.

Jack asks Kate if she's ever used a needle. When Jack explains that he needs her to use a needle and thread to stitch his wound, she balks at the idea, but Jack convinces her that she can do it. Kate is looking a little woozy sewing up Jack. She threatens to throw-up. Jack reassures her with a surgery story about being afraid and how he made a choice to let fear in, to let it ravage him, but only for five seconds. He slowly counted to five and then went back to his work as a doctor.

That night survivors are gathered around the signal fire and smaller fires littered about the beach after sunset. Jack and Kate look over a man wearing a suit and his injuries, a large piece of shrapnel protruding from his chest. Kate asks if the man is going to live and Jack suspects there's something to the question. When he asks if Kate knows the wounded man, she only says that she was seated next to him.

A little later they sit by the fire talking about the crash.. Jack guesses they were a forty-thousand feet when they hit the first bit of turbulence. He imagines they might have hit an air pocket and dropped maybe 200 feet. Jack points out that neither the tail nor the cockpit are on the beach, but if they could find the cockpit they might be able to get the transceiver and send out a message. Kate notes that she saw smoke in the valley and if Jack's going to look for the cockpit, then she's coming with him. Suddenly, a terrible and indescribable sound rises up from the mountains central to the island.

All of the survivors rise, they're attention caught and fear rising. The sound gets closer and a thunderous stomp announces that whatever it is, it's getting closer. There's movement in the bushes and trees fall in the wake of whatever is striding through the jungle.

In the morning the survivors speculate about the sound, but no one has a good guess. Rose swears it sounds "familiar" but still can't place it. Jack is on his way to look for the cockpit, but insists that Kate should stay behind. Kate won't hear of it and Jack acquiesces, but notes that she needs better shoes. Kate finds better shoes, but they're still on a corpse and. Charlie asks to come along as well.

As the three walk into the jungle, Kate asks Charlie if she knows him from somewhere. Charlie is thrilled to reveal he was or rather is, the bass player in Drive Shaft. The band is in the middle of a comeback.

It isn't long before it starts to rain. The three explorers trudge along. Back at the beach everyone is taking cover with the exception of Locke. Locke has his face and hands turned toward the heavens, welcoming the downpour.

Jack, Kate and Charlie find the cockpit and the three of them climb into the plane, which is precariously perched at a steep angle. Inside the cockpit the co-pilot is dead, but Kate and Jack find the pilot still alive. Charlie seems to have disappeared somewhere.

The pilot shares the information that the radio went out six hours into the flight. They had turned to head for Fiji and were a thousand miles off course when they crashed. Rescuers will be looking in the wrong place. The pilot tells them where the transceiver is and a roaring animalistic sound fills the plane and it shifts.

. Jack tries to look out the remaining glass of the cockpit windows. The pilot takes it one step further and leans out through the broken glass, pushing aside branches for a better look. The plane trembles and whatever is outside wrenches the pilot kicking and screaming out with it.

Jack manages to grab the transceiver despite the fact that it rolls away with the shifting plane. The three jump outside where the rain is still a downpour and run for their lives. The "monster" doesn't appear but the three of them make a gruesome find. It's the mangled body of the pilot in the jungle canopy. No one wants to comprehend how that might have happened.

Oceanic Flight #815 101
Who was where on flight #815 part one.

Jack is staring out of the airplane's window when a flight attendant stops to check on him and the drink he's ordered.

Jack is obviously less than impressed with the quality of his cocktail and the stewardess slips him two more bottles of liquor. One of which he puts into his drink and he pockets the other. He gulps down his drink and stands to try and get out of his seat. Charlie rushes by him on his way to the lavatory, stopping him. Jack sits down in the seat close to the aisle and the plane hits turbulence. Looking across the aisle, he notices Rose and she seems nervous. He tries to comfort her and promises to keep her company until her husband comes back. Then suddenly the plane drops, tossing passengers from the floor to the ceiling and back. Alarms sound, masks drop and Jack puts his on.

Analyze This

Jack as Hero: Jack is the perfect example of "hero" as in Joseph Campbell's description of an archetypal hero's journey. Jack is drawn in by the "call to duty" as a reluctant hero, but will he rise to the occasion?

Pristine Beach: Jack runs to find the source of the crash-site cacophony, but first stumble upon pristine beach.

Could this foreshadow the deception of the island, a place where nothing is as it seems upon first glance?

Signs & Symbols

- **Ocean-** All life originated in the ocean. Especially in Jungian interpretation, this is a place of creativity, fertility, and birth. In order to get home, the survivors will somehow have to cross the ocean or symbolically go back to their origin.

- **Rain-** rain is a symbol of rebirth. The rainstorm symbolizes the rebirth of the survivors as all is washed clean or simply away. This is especially true for Locke.

- **Jungle** – As in the Joseph Conrad's "Heart of Darkness" the jungle symbolized mystery and the origin of man. Somewhere in the primordial interior of the jungle might lay the secrets to mankind. The choice to continue the journey will involve exploring the ocean or the jungle and it will be personal one for each of the survivors.

Listen to What the Fans Say

Some fans speculate that everyone on the plane died and those that survived are now in purgatory being given the opportunity to right their wrongs and move on. Perhaps those that die on the show, such as the pilot and the other passengers are actually being revived on earth and snatched from purgatory. Could the survivors be winning their way to heaven and sealing their fate in hell?

Truth & Speculation

- For the sake of safety the wing of the plane (which nearly falls on Claire and Hurley) was held up by a tremendous crane that had to be digitized out of the picture.

- The scene where Kate sews up Jack's wound was the scene that was used for both actors' auditions.

- The tattoos on Matthew Fox are real and the line about "counting to five" was in the script before he was cast as Jack.

- Sawyer, who will have much to say later, never says a word in part one of the pilot episode.

Quotable Quips

- **Kate:** (on stitching Jack's wound) Any color preference?

- **Charlie:**(on the introduction of the "monster") Terrific.

- **Charlie:** (on the sudden downpour) Hey guys, is this normal? This kind of day turning into night, you know... end of the world type weather? Is this... guys?

- **Sawyer:** (on what the "monster" might be) Sure it's monkeys. It's monkey island.

Sawyerisms

None in this episode.

Seven Degrees of LOST

- **Charlie's** rush for the bathroom stops **Jack** from leaving the area where he's sitting.
- **Jack** sits next to **Rose** because of the sudden turbulence.

Episode Two: Pilot Part 2

Summary

When Jack, Kate and Charlie return with the receiver they find Sawyer and Sayid fighting on the beach, Sawyer accusing the other man of being a terrorist. Michael presents a pair of handcuffs to Jack that Walt found in the jungle while looking for Vincent. There was obviously someone dangerous on the plane. Kate puts a stop to the fisticuffs and asks if anyone knows how to fix the transceiver they found in the cockpit. Charlie, Jack and Kate don't reveal about the pilot being killed by the "monster" only that no one survived from the front of the plane. Sayid believes he can fix the transceiver and reveals to Hurley that he was a member of the Republican Guard, the Iraqi forces during the Gulf War.

Kate checks on the man in the suit who was seriously wounded and finds that Jack is preparing to remove the piece of shrapnel. Kate tells Jack that Sayid has fixed the transceiver, but they need to hike to the highest point of the Island to make sure they have a signal. Jack is busy with his patient and tells Kate to run if she sees anything.

After chastising his wife for having the top button of her shirt undone, Jin gathers sea urchin for food. His slaps his wife's hand away when she tries to take a bite and instead walks off with the tray to offer the food to the other survivors. Hurley declines the offer. However, Claire eventually gives in and tries a bite. She doesn't seem convinces that she likes it, but suddenly her baby kicks. She hasn't felt the baby moves since before the plane crashed. She is ecstatic and pulls Jin's hand to her belly to felt he baby kick.

Walt reads a Green Lantern/Flash comic book, at least he looks at the pictures. The words are in Spanish, but the drawings are of the heroes fighting with a polar bear. Michael asks him if he can read Spanish, trying to start a conversation. Walt tells him that he can't, and that he found the comic. Knowing that Walt is upset about not being able to find his dog, Michael makes the mistake of offering to buy a new dog to replace Vincent when they get home. Walt is furious and storms off.

Walt comes across Locke playing a board game and asked if its checkers. Locke explains it's better, it's backgammon. It's the oldest game in the world, two players, two sides, one is light the other dark. Then Locke asks Walt if he wants to know a secret.

Boone and Shannon argue over the fact that Shannon hasn't helped with anything since they crashed. They are brother and sister and fight like it. Boone calls her "worthless" and Shannon demands to go on the hike in order to prove that she's not. Charlie says that he's going as well, but from the look on his face it's just to follow Shannon. Sawyer is wrapped up reading a letter that is obviously painful, but joins the hiking party before they leave.

On the walk to the might point, the group is followed and then attacked. As everyone runs away, Sawyer stays behind and shoots their attacker. It's a bear, but more than that, it's a polar. The group doesn't spend much time pondering the bear, but instead immediately worries over where Sawyer got the gun. Kate disarms him deftly and then oddly asks how to break the gun down as if she has no experience. Sawyer professes that he took the gun and a badge off a U.S. Marshal that was on the plane.

The man in the suit, who we now know was the Marshall, is in bad shape. With Hurley's poor assistance, Jack removes the shrapnel. While Hurley is passed out from the sight of blood and Jack is working feverishly to stop the bleeding, the man regains consciousness. He immediately starts asking for his prisoner.

Meanwhile, the hiking party has gotten a signal and more than that a transmission, only it's in French. Shannon, with a year's worth of schooling in France attempts to translate and she doesn't like what she hears. The woman is saying something to the effect of "Please help me. Please come. I'm alone now on the island. They others are dead. It killed them all." As the transmission repeats, a mechanical voice end the message with a number, on higher each. Sayid does the calculations and tells them that it's been playing over and over for sixteen years.

Oceanic Flight 815 101
Who was where on Flight #815 Part Two

Charlie is seated on the plane fiddling with a ring on his finger and tapping it on the arm of the chair. He is obviously agitated and a flight attendant checks on him, but he sends her away. While the flight attendants are huddled together talking, Charlie unsnaps his seatbelt, jumps up and runs for the lavatory. He bumps into Jack and then Shannon as the flight attendants chase after him. Charlie makes it to the bathroom, locks himself inside where he snorts heroine from a small bag that was in his pocket. The attendants are now bagging on the door, demanding he come out because the turbulence has started. Charlie drops the drugs in the toilet, but doesn't get a chance to flush them. The plane suddenly drops, throwing him to the ceiling. Thrown from the bathroom, he manages to get into a seat, buckle in and put on the oxygen mask as the plane goes down.

Kate is handcuffed and sitting with the U.S. Marshal on the plane who seems to take great joy in tormenting her over her chained state. She is about to ask him a favor when the plane suddenly drops. A heavy suitcase flies out of the overhead bin, hitting the Marshal on the head and knocking him out. The masks come down, but Kate is unable to reach hers because of the cuffs. She gets the key out of the Marshal's pocket, unlocks her cuffs and pulls a mask to her face, taking a breath. Then she secures the mask on the Marshal and reaches for her own. As she holds her mask to her face the tail end of the airplane rips away, debris and passengers disappearing out the back.

Analyze This
Backgammon: Locke introduces Walt to backgammon, an ancient game where one player is represented by white

pieces and the other player by dark pieces. It's a game of strategy, number and luck, much like the game everyone is engaged in on this island. Each character will face their "shadow" side in order to move forward. Like backgammon, the game doesn't advance without both the light and the dark sides playing. Who's playing what side?

Polar Bear: We see a polar bear first in the comic, attacking the comic heroes in the book that Walt is reading. A live and ferocious polar bear attacks our heroes shortly after. What is the significance? Do all fears come to life on the island?

Signs & Symbols

- **Handcuffs-** Are both a symbol of protection and of restraint. Whatever was once handcuffed and is now loose could be very dangerous. Whoever was wearing them is now free and no longer a prisoner. Everyone on the island is going to face what has been freed in themselves. They are no longer prisoners to their past lives, but the part of them that has been freed may also be dangerous.

- **Gun**- Whoever holds the gun holds the power, the power to protect and to destroy. Whoever is responsible the gun will be the leader and depended on to use the weapon justly or suffer the consequences.

- **Gift of food:** Jin offers Claire some food and her baby comes to life. Sea urchin is traditionally eaten raw or slightly cooked and considered an aphrodisiac. Is it this food of fertility that brings the baby to stir?

Listen to What the Fans Say –

Some fans speculate that those that are on the island are the passengers that put on their oxygen masks as the plane was going down. Was there something in the masks? Jack passed out and didn't see a thing, but Kate put her mask on late and watched the plane break apart. If all those wearing the masks were drugged, is it possibly that the crash wasn't a crash at all, but rather a careful orchestration?

Truth & Speculation

- Jack was supposed to die in the second act of the first episode, not the pilot of the plane. The plan was to have Kate be the "hero."

- This is what Jin is saying to Claire in Korean when he offers her food and the baby kicks: *This is sun gae, try some please. You have to eat for the baby, try at least one. This one, eat this one." Claire eats a piece How is that? Good? Eat one more.*

  Claire's baby suddenly starts moving after she eats a piece and she tries to get Jin to feel the baby move. Jin says *Are you OK? No, no, no, don't do this. No, no, no. Please let my hand go*

- Josh Holloway was told to imagine he was reading a suicide note during the scene where he reads the "letter."

Quotable Quips

- **Shannon** (to Boone): I've just been through a trauma here, okay?
- **Sawyer** (to Kate): I'm a complex guy, sweetheart.
- **Locke** (to Walt): Walt...do you want to know a secret?
- **Sawyer** (to Kate's question about where the bear came from) Probably bear village. How the hell do I know?
- **Charlie** (on hearing the French transmission) It's French. The French are coming. I've never been so happy to hear French.

Sawyerisms

- **To Hurley:** Lardo

- **To Sayid:** Chief

- **To Shannon:** Sweetcheeks

- **To Kate:** Sweetheart

Seven Degrees of LOST

Boone and **Shannon** are step-siblings

Charlie knocks into **Shannon** when he runs for the bathroom.

Kate is the **Marshal's** prisoner

Episode Three: Tabula Rasa

Summary

The Marshal wakes again and asks Jake where his handcuffs are. He also tells Jack to check his jacket pocket. Inside is a mug shot of Kate. The Marshall tells him that she's dangerous and not to trust her. It isn't long after that when Hurley finds the mug shot too. Hack insists that it's none of their business.

The group who heard the transmission returns with the transceiver and little information for most of the group other than that they couldn't send out a signal. Sayid organizes the other survivors to gather the electronic equipment that might be used to boost a signal and to prepare for rationing food and water. In the mean time Kate pulls Jack aside and tells him what they heard. Although Kate asks about the Marshal, Jack tells her he hasn't said anything.

Jack searches for antibiotics to help the Marshal who's getting worse. Sawyer points out that the doctor may be wasting precious medication on a dead man, but Jack won't relent. Later that evening Kate sneaks into the medical tent and stands over the Marshal, staring into his sleeping face. He wakes suddenly and grabs her by the throat. Jack walks in to find the man choking her and pulls him off of her.

Kate asks if the Marshal is okay and Jack lets her know he's dying, but can't bring himself to say it exactly. Kate gets Jack to admit the man is going to suffer and suggests that he put him out of his misery. Jack revels what he's learned about her and shuts her down by noting that He's not a murderer.

Michael is having a hard time with Walt, who's still sullen about missing his dog. Michael also doesn't approve of his burgeoning friendship with Locke. He promises to look for Vincent, which he does but almost immediately gets chased by something in the jungle. Running away he stumbles on a half-naked Sun and an awkward situation.

Locke in the meantime makes a high-pitched whistle to try to call the dog to him. When he retrieves the dog, he finds Michael and gives the man the opportunity to bring the dog back to his son himself.

The Marshal is getting worse and his moans are making the whole camp uncomfortable. Sawyer suggests to Kate that she should end his misery, after all, she's the one carrying the gun now. The Marshal compounds the situation by asking to talk to Kate. What he wants to know about the favor she was going to ask before the plane crash. Kate reluctantly tells him she wanted to make sure that Ray Mullen got his reward money. Knowing that he's going to die, the Marshal asks Kate if she's going to put him out of his misery.

Kate can't bring herself to do it, but leaves the chore to Sawyer, who fails. Sawyer's shot to the chest misses the heart and instead perforates a lung, merely making the death worse and longer. Sawyer is out of bullets and horrified, but

Jack is furious. Now the doctor has no choice, he disappears inside the tent and finishes the job himself.

Kate wants to tell Jack what she did, but Jack doesn't want to hear it. As far as Jack is concerned, they are all starting over.

Kate Austin 101

A farmer in Australia, Ray Mullen, finds Kate sleeping in his sheep pen. He wakes her with a shotgun in her face and can't get a straight answer from her about what she's doing there or who she got to his place in the middle of nowhere. She tells him her name is Annie and he offers her a meal. After revealing that his wife is dead, Kate agrees to work for him on the farm.

Kate works for Ray for almost three months and is about to walk out on him in the middle of the night, when he catches her collecting her earnings from a hiding place in the pantry. Ray seems hurt and is able to talk Kate into staying one more night so that he can drive her to the train station in the morning.

On the drive in to the train station, Kate realizes that Ray is nervous and looking for something and figures out what's going on. He admits he saw her picture in a post office and turned her in for the bounty. He's apologetic, but really needed the money for the mortgage and the reward is $23,000. On cue, the Marshall shows up driving beside them.

Desperate to get away Kate struggles with Ray for the wheel and in the struggle crashes the car. Ray is unconscious and the engine is on fire. Kate pulls Ray out of harm's way, using all her strength to drag him clear of the wreck. Taking the time to do this gives the Marshal a chance to catch up and take her into custody.

Analyze This

- **Killing the Marshall**: Jack has done everything in his power to try to save the Marshal, despite the fact that he was most likely a "waste" of antibiotics. Jack has an inability to "let things go" and look at the big picture. Perhaps this first test of doing what is right for the group instead of for his personal morality is the beginning of Jack as the leader?

- **Charlie's taped fingers**: Initially Charlie taped his fingers and wrote "FATE" across the tape. In this episode he wrote "LATE." Does simply mean the rescue party is late? Or perhaps now that he has found his drugs again, he thinks it's too late for him?

Signs & Symbols
- **Ray Mullen's prosthetic arm:** The prosthesis that Ray Mullen wears is not obvious at first glance, but signifies a person that is not completely whole. Although Kate is apparently missing a piece of her soul, rather than her body, perhaps she finds herself relating to this man because like her he isn't complete.

He parallels her as a broken person that can make decisions both with their conscience and through necessity. He illuminates who Kate is so the audience has a better view.

- **Antibiotics:** As the medicines available to the doctor dwindle they represent all the is left of modern society and of how the survivors know to survive. They will have to use their ingenuity as medicine now.

- **Man's best friend:** Vincent the Labrador retriever might have survived in the forest because he is a dog and therefore would not succumb to the "illusions" of the island. The dog represents seeing things for what they are and becomes a protector for the survivors.

Listen to What the Fans Say –

What exactly is going on between the Marshal and Kate? Is it just that he is a sadistic jerk, or does their relationship go further? Fans point out that the Marshall asked Jack if "she got to him too." Were they romantically involved? That might explain his cruelty toward her. Or perhaps he was just a man posing as a Marshal and part of a bigger plan to get Kate on the plane?

Truth & Speculation

- Tabula Rasa means "blank slate." It is theory developed by John Locke, a real 17ᵗʰ century English philosopher. Tabula rasa is the notion that human beings are born "blank" (with no built-in mental content), and that their identity is defined entirely by events after birth. If everyone on LOST has now been reborn, then they are all blank slates creating new destinies.

- The LOST team had a tough time finding the perfect actress to play. They knew though, that had the right girl the minute they saw Evangeline Lilly. However, she is a Canadian actress and they had to get the proper paperwork through before she could work. No one was certain she would be the actress playing the role. Her visa came through just in time. They were shooting the next day.

- The dog that plays Vincent is actually a female and her name is Madison.

Quotable Quips

- **Hurley** (to Jack about the monster): So how do you know it wasn't a dinosaur?

- **Jack** (to Kate): Three days ago we all died. We should all be able to start over.

- **Sawyer** (to Sayid drawing diagrams in the dirt) Nice stick.

- **Sawyer** (In reply to Jack's question of "what's in the bag?") Booze, smokes, a couple *Playboys*. What's in yours?

Sawyerisms

- **To Sayid:** Abdul

- **To Sayid:** Al Jazeera

- **To Kate:** Freckles

Seven Degrees of LOST

Kate was befriended by **Ray Mullen** and then turned in by him.

Episode Four: Walkabout

Summary

Vincent begins barking in the middle of the night waking all the survivors to the sound of something rummaging through the fuselage. Everyone is terrified, but Sawyer and Jack enter with flashlights to investigate. Startled, the creatures inside the plane stampede, nearly running everyone over. They are boars.

Knowing that the boars are most likely feeding on the remains of those that didn't survive, Jack tells everyone that something must be done. The bodies must be burnt because burying isn't a logical solution. Sayid disagrees, feeling that this is disrespectful to the dead. Still, Jack insists that everyone begin to gather firewood and to plan on burning the fuselage after sundown. This way the fire can do double-duty as a signal fire.

As Sawyer and Hurley fight over the last of the peanuts, the survivors come to a horrible realization, there's no food left. As panic begins to bubble up, Locke steps in dramatically throwing a knife into a tree with precision and stating that they will hunt boar.

Michael decides to go with Locke on the hunt and leaves Walt with Sun. Kate goes on the boar hunt as well, but has ulterior motives. Sayid is working on creating antennae that can be mounted on different parts of the island in order to triangulate the French woman's transmission. There is likely a power source there.

The survivors decide to do a sort of memorial service for those in the fuselage and Claire assumes that Jack will lead it. Jack chafes at being placed in the role of assumed leader and Claire decides to do it herself. He again gets irritated when Boone asks him to talk to Rose who's been sitting by herself in silence and apathy since the crash and apparent loss of her husband.

Although Jack complains that he's not a psychiatrist, he goes to talk to Rose. It takes a little effort, but she finally speaks to Jack and agrees to rejoin the others in a bit. As they continue to sit and talk, Rose reveals that she is certain her husband is still alive even though he was in the back of the plane. Jack expression is of compassion, but disbelief. Then he sees a man in a dark suit staring at him from a distance. Rose doesn't see him and Jack seems unnerved.

As a result of an argument with Boone about being able to take care of herself, Shannon charms Charlie into attempting to catch fish for her. Charlie enlists Hurley to help, but neither of them are having much luck trying to spear a fish out of the ocean. When at last Charlie does spear one, he brings it beaming back to Shannon. Boone is disgusted with his sister's manipulation of yet another man.

Out in the jungle, the hunters are able to track the boar, but Michael startles it. Locke and Kate get out of the way, but Michael gets knocked to the ground, a gash in his leg. He's injured too badly to continue the hunt. Locke tell Kate to take him back to camp while Locke continues the boar hunt. Kate protests, telling him he can't. Locke mutters under his breathe, "Don't tell me what I can't do."

Kate walks Michael back, helping him take the weight off of his injured leg. She asks to stop at a tree to climb up and attach the antennae from Sayid. When she reaches the top she suddenly hears the tell-tale sound of trees breaking and a low growling. Startled she drops the antennae, breaking it. The grasses are moving back where they came from. Something is heading for Locke. Locke runs right into it and stares up into the thing's eyes with rapture, while it looks down on him.

Back at the camp the survivors prepare for the memorial service at evening. While gathering personal affects, Clair finds an envelope with a photo of woman that belongs to Sayid. She gives it back to him. Sawyer brings Claire a handful of wallets, obviously embarrassed. Michael and Kate have returned and everyone is fearing the worst for Locke. They shouldn't though, Locke returns with boar in hand.

The survivors all stand around the fire as Claire reads off names and facts gleaned from the possessions of those that have died. Jack sits on the shore away from the fire, staring out into the sea. Within the fire a wheel burns and John Locke smiles.

John Locke 101

Locke sits at a desk and answers his phone. He has a cryptic conversion with someone he calls GL-12 and who calls him Colonel Locke. They agree to meet a rendezvous point at thirteen hundred hours. Then Locke's boss appears behind him and chastises him for not finishing some TPS reports.

At lunch Locke plays a board game with toy army soldiers. Randy comes over to harass him, noting that Locke isn't really a "colonel" at all. Then he asks him what a "walkabout" is, reading from a brochure he has snatched from Locke's desk. Randy torments him, not believing that Locke is capable of undertaking such an adventure. Under his breath Locke says, 'Don't tell me what I can't do.

On the phone at home Locke tells Helen, a woman he talks to like a love interest, that he has told off Randy and is going on the walkabout. He has also bought a ticket for her. She doesn't react well, stating she's not allowed to meet customers. She hangs up on him, uncomfortable with the situation and worried that he will spend another $89.95 if they talk any longer.

Locke makes it to Australia, but in the office of the travel agent, with the bus waiting outside he get the biggest letdown of all. They won't let him go on the walkabout because he's in a wheelchair. Locke argues that he's prepared, the lived with his condition for four years and that it's destiny, but to no avail. The bus leaves without him as he shouts, "Don't tell me what I can't do.

Analyze This

Opening eyes: Many scenes begin with a close-up of the character's eye opening. The eye is the window to the soul, so perhaps this is indicative of the journey the viewer is about to take in looking into the soul of this character. They eye is also a symbol of knowledge. The Serpent promised Adam and Eve that their eyes would "be opened" if they ate of the fruit of the tree of knowledge of good and evil. Every survivor is truly having their "eyes opened" and are symbolically eating from the "tree of knowledge."

Locke survives: What happened with the monster? Is it possible that it didn't see Locke and he was able to escape? Or perhaps whatever it is it chose not to destroy Locke and let him leave. The real John Locke writes in "An Essay Concerning Human Understanding" from 1690 that "The visible marks of extraordinary wisdom and power appear so plainly in all the works of creation that a rational creature who will but seriously reflect on them cannot miss the discovery of a diety." This basically means that a person who stares at anything in nature, even a tree, might find God. Perhaps there's no real Lostzilla at all, just whatever the island feels you need to see.

Signs & Symbols

- **Staring into the face of the "monster":** Locke looks into the "Heart of Darkness" and finds it beautiful. Looking into the darkness is often a symbol of seeing your "shadow side" and owning it. A person has to be both dark and light in order to be whole. This scene may symbolize the completion of Locke becoming whole.

- **Regaining mobility:** For Locke to be able to walk after the crash and after four years of being bound to a wheelchair is a miracle. This miracle represents the strange and wonderful possibilities of the island.

- **Boars:** The boars symbolize a means of sustenance and food is a very important motif on LOST. All the survivors must find new way to get the sustenance they need both physically and metaphorically.

- **Strategy Games:** Locke's previous life is fulfilled through fantasy strategy games. Playing Axis/Allies foreshadows the strategist that Locke will become on the island.

Listen to What the Fans Say

Some fans argue that although Locke spent what must have been a great deal of time reading up on the appropriate skills for his walkabout, this isn't enough to account for all he knows. How does Locke know how to hunt boar, throw knives and carve a whistle to call a dog? He also seems to know more about the other survivors than they know about themselves. Is it possible that Locke is something more than he seems? Is it possible that Locke is evil or a minion of the island's darkness?

Truth & Speculation

- All of Locke's flashbacks in this episode are intentionally missing the colors blue and green.

- The machine next to Locke's bed is a Transcutaneous Electrical Nerve Stimulator meant for muscle therapy.

- This episode was at one point called, "Lord of the Files" before it was renamed to "Walkabout"

- Norman Croucher never actually climbed Mt. Everest. This was a mistake made by the writers.

Quotable Quips

- **John Locke** (says three times): Don't tell me what I can't do.

- **Sawyer** (to Jack regarding hunting boars) Better than the 3 of you wandering into the magic forest to bag a hunk of ham with nothing but a little bitty hunting knife? Hell no, it's the best idea I ever heard.

- **Shannon** (to Boone) What's a four letter word for I don't care?

- **Shannon** (to Boone): Oh, go rescue a baby bird or something.

- **Hurley** (to everyone regarding Locke) Who is this guy?

Sawyerisms

- **To Boone:** Metro

- **To Hurley:** Pork Pie

- **To Kate:** The Mighty Huntress

- **Naming the Jungle:** Jungle of Mystery; Magic Forest

Seven Degrees of LOST

Randy is **John Locke's** boss at the box company.

Helen is **John Locke's** love interest.

Episode Five: White Rabbit

Summary

One of the survivors, Joanna, goes out for a morning swim and gets caught in a riptide. Charlie finds Jack to save her because Charlie can't swim. When Jack tries to rescue her he finds Boone instead. Boone had swam out, trying to rescue the woman himself, but has become another victim of the ocean. Jack takes Boone back to shore, thinking that he can still get out in time to rescue the woman, but when he gets back out he can't find her. He agonizes over what he thinks was a bad decision and again sees a man in a dark suit standing in the water. When he tries to point the man out to Kate, he has already disappeared. Kate worries that Jack hasn't had enough sleep.

Hurley points out to Jack that the remaining water is minimal, eighteen bottles. It's not enough for the 46 survivors. Charlie continues on this theme by noting that there's not enough boar to feed everyone either. As the two act like advisors to a leader, Jack brushes them off. He doesn't want to be the leader. This is compounded by Boone chastising him for not saving the woman who drowned.

Jack doesn't pay any attention to Boone. The man in the black suit is on the beach again. Jack run after the man and catches up to him. When he reaches out to touch the man's shoulder, he turns. Jack asks, "Dad?" Then his father disappears.

Jin and Sun discuss their situation. Jin is trying to take care of her and notes that she needs more water. Sun wants to try to communicate with the other survivors. Jin insists that they don't need anyone else and that he will take care of her. Sawyer is hoarding and bartering with goods that he has procured off of the plane. When Claire passes out from the heat and needs water, everyone discovers that the water supply is missing. Jin and Sawyer are the first two suspects, but nothing can be proven. Locke goes into the jungle to look for more water for the survivors.

Meanwhile, Jack continues the mad chase after his father through the jungle. He trips and tumbles off the side of a hill following him and clings to the roots of a plant, a long fall beneath him. Locke appears and saves him falling to his death.

Locke tells Jack that the others need him, that they need a leader. Jack tells him that he doesn't have what it takes. Locke asks what he's in the jungle looking for and Jack explains that what he's looking for is a hallucination, a white rabbit. Locke is sure that there's more to it than that. He thinks there's something strange and mystical about the island. Locke tells Jack to keep following his "white rabbit" and disappears.

Jack does continue to follow the vision of his father and it leads him further into the jungle. He reaches caves and running water. There is also debris from the plane crash. More importantly, Jack finds the coffin that his father was in. When he opens it however, he finds it empty. Angry, Jack smashes the coffin with a pipe.

When Jack returns, the survivors have discovered that Boone stole the water in an attempt to take responsibility. Jack stands up as a leader and tells everyone that he has found a water source and that it's time for everyone to come to terms with the fact that they may not be rescued. Whoever doesn't want to come with him to get water should find another way to contribute. Everyone needs to start working together.

Jack Shepard 101

Jack as a young boy gets beaten up because he chooses to protect his friend Marc Silverman. His father, Christian Shephard is very disappointed in him because he was defending someone other than himself. His father is doctor and tells him that he lost a boy on his operating table just that day. He says it was his responsibility to make the decisions and sometimes he fails, but he has what it takes to deal with it. Jack should never try to be a hero because he can't save everyone and when he fails he doesn't have what it takes.

As an adult Jack has become estranged from his father. They haven't been on speaking terms for two months. His mother, Margo, tells him that his father has left and he has to go find him. She seethes that after what Jack did there is no other choice but to go to Australia and bring his father home.

In Australia Jack tracks his father's trail, but he hasn't used the bed in his hotel room in the past three days. His father also left his wallet. The concierge tells Jack politely that his father has been on a bender since he's been there.

Where Jack ultimately finds his father is in the morgue. The man has basically drunk himself to death. Now charged with getting the body home so that there can be a funeral, Jack has a hard time getting the airline to clear putting his father on the plane. He begs the ticket agent to get his father on the plane so that it can all be over.

Analyze This

The Casket: Why was Christian's coffin empty? Could the body of Jack's father have fallen out of the coffin during the crash? If it had would somehow have already found it? Then does this mean that the body was never in the coffin and didn't make it on the plane or that Jack's father is truly walking about the island? Whatever the truth is, it seems to be a metaphor for the unfinished business in Jack's life. Will Jack ever be able to bury his father and rid himself of his ghosts?

If he jumped off a cliff would you?: Jack is willing to follow the vision of his father off a precipice, a move that symbolizes how Jack followed his father throughout his life. Jack doesn't believe he is a leader because this is what his father has taught him. Staying in the shadow of a father figure is all Jack knows to do. Now that Locke has saved him by pulling him back up from the edge of the cliff, will Jack be able to find his own way?

Signs & Symbols

Riptide: The riptide that carries Joanna away to her death represents the unpredictability of the island and life for survivors. The ocean gives sustenance, but the ocean also takes away. Something as simple as a morning swim can cause death and the survivors need to learn to be on their toes.

Water: Water is one of the basic needs of survival. Whoever has the water is the island's provider. Although Jack refuses to take responsibility for the water, in the end he is the one who discovers a new source and provides. In this way, being the water bearer symbolizes Jack as a born leader.

Coffin: A coffin represents the end and the ritual of putting someone or something to rest. This is a ritual that Jack desperately needs but is unable to finish because his father's coffin is empty.

Listen to What the Fans Say

Fans note that Claire looks through at least 20 suitcases and doesn't find a hairbrush. If the plane crash was staged, it is quite possible that in packing the suitcases belonging to supposed passengers, hairbrushes might have been forgotten. Chances are most travelers carrying luggage pack a hairbrush. So why are there none on the plane? Perhaps this is one more clue to the fact that someone is behind the "crash" and somehow orchestrating the entire scenario.

Truth & Speculation

- The cast and crew call Matthew Fox "Foxy"

- The plane on the beach is a real plane from a airline graveyard out in the Mojave desert

- Sawyer is reading Watership Down, a book about rabbits and the main character's name is Fiver.

Quotable Quips

- **Hurley** (regarding the water shortage): Maybe we can make on of those water-finding sticks.

- **Sayid** (regarding the missing water): You go after him now, he'll give you nothing. But if you wait, a rabbit will always lead you down the hole.

- **Sawyer** (throwing Kate the Marshal's badge): Seeing as how you're the new sheriff in town, might as well make it official.

- **Locke** (to Jack) I've looked into the eye of this island and what I saw was beautiful.

- **Jack** (to everyone) If we can't live together...we're gonna die alone.

Sawyerisms

- **To Shannon**: Sticks

- **About Jin**: Mr. Miyagi

- **To Kate**: Freckles

Seven Degrees of LOST

- **Jack** is the son of **Christian Shephard.**

- **Jin** is standing behind **Jack** in line when he argues with the airline employee about getting his father's body on the plane.

Episode Six: House of the Rising Sun

Summary

With surprising rage Jin attacks Michael and even though Walt yells for him to stop, Jin continues to pound the other man. Sayid and Sawyer come running at the cries and Sayid tackles Jin. Sawyer and Sayid handcuff Jin to a piece of the plane wreckage. Sayid asks what happened, insinuating that Michael must have instigated the fight. Michael insists he has no idea what provoked the attack.

Outside of the caves gathering water, Charlie steps into a hive of bees. Locke tells him to stand still or he'll split the hive, but Charlie has an irrational fear of bees. Before they have a chance to cover the hive and get Charlie out of danger, Charlie takes a step and the cracks open the combs, releasing the bees. Jack, Kate, Locke and Charlie run for cover. Jack and Kate find themselves inside the caves and make a gruesome discovery. The bodies and a man and woman some forty years dead have been laid to rest inside the cave. Next to one of the bodies is a bag holding a black and a white stone. Jack pockets the stones when Charlie and Locke enter the cave.

Kate and Jack load up on water and take it back to camp, discussing the possibility of bringing everyone to the caves for shelter and water. Jack is convinced it's the best way to keep everyone safe, but knows that many are not going to want to leave the shore and the possibility of a rescue boat. Kate isn't convinced.

Sayid isn't convinced that moving away from the shore is a good idea. He feels it's giving up. Jack goes to work talking to the other survivors, while Sayid goes to Michael to tell him others are considering the move. Michael agrees to stay on the beach as well.

Back at the cave Charlie and Locke are looking through the debris from the crash, searching for useful items. Locke won't let Charlie out of his sight which is making it hard for Charlie to get a fix. Finally, Locke softens Charlie up by telling him he knows who he is and asking him how much he misses his guitar. Locke tells Charlie that he's going to run out of drugs eventually and if he quits now, at least it will be his choice. Maybe if he sacrifices something to the island, the island will give him back his guitar. Charlie hands Locke the last of his drugs and Locke shows Charlie the guitar case above them, hung up on some roots on the outer cave wall.

Sun approaches Michael and surprises him by speaking English. She explains that even her husband doesn't know she can speak English and that what happened between them was a misunderstanding. Michael is wearing a watch that belonged to her father, that getting it back is a matter of honor.

Michael goes to Jin and gives him back his watch then cuts the handcuffs free of the plane with an axe. Michael tells Jin to stay away from him and his son then walks away. Jin and Sun join Hurley and the others who have gone to the caves. Kate, Michael, Walt and Sayid have stayed behind.

Sun Kwon 101

Jin serves Sun at a party where she is an honored guest and he is the waiter. When he gets her alone, it is obvious that they are in a relationship. Sun was to run away to America to elope, but Jin wants a respectable marriage. The problem is convincing Sun's father, a very powerful man to give them his blessing. Jin says that he will make Sun's father understand and hands her a flower.

Jin makes good on his promise to win Sun's hand. He must take a year of management training and work a year in the factory, but he has convinced the man to let him marry his daughter. Sun is worried, but can't help but be joyous over the ring he presents her.

Married, Jin and Sun seem to doing well financially. Sun has been out shopping and Jin presents her with a puppy. It's a sweet gesture, but then the phone rings and Jin is called to duty by Sun's father. When he returns there's blood all over his hands and clothes. Sun wants to know what Jin does for her father, she's knows it's bad. Jin can only tell her that he does as he is told and does it for the benefit of their relationship.

As Jin gets more sullen and withdrawn, Sun is obviously formulating a plan. A woman who has supposedly come to talk to her about decorating the apartment asks her if she really wants to go through with the plan. Sun's husband and father will do everything they can to find her. Sun has taken English lessons and is certain she wants to escape. The decorator tells her that in the airport at eleven fifteen she is to make an excuse and walk out of the airport. A car will be waiting and her family will assume she was kidnapped. When she isn't found they will assume she is dead and she will be free. The decorator leaves her with a passport, telling Sun to repeat the designated time.

At the airport Sun struggles to leave her husband. The time has come, but when he looks to her and smiles, a white flower in his hand, she makes up her mind. She joins him in line at the ticket counter and takes the flower from him.

Analyze This

Black and White: Black and white is a recurring theme in LOST. Jack's father wears a black suit with white shoes, Sun holds a white flower, backgammon is played with black and white pieces, and then there are the black and white stones with Adam and Eve. The producers say they know exactly who Adam and Eve are and why they had those stones. What is the significance of black & white? Is it simply good and evil playing out on the island, the fact that all characters display duality, or is it something far more complex?

Jack Hides the Stones: Why does Jack hide the black and white stones when Locke enters the cave? He very purposefully puts the stones back into the pouch and pockets them, taking care that Locke doesn't see. Does Jack know the significance of the stones? And if so, why does he want them to remain a secret from Locke?

Signs & Symbols

The stones: Black and white stones called Urim and Thummin are used to answer yes or no questions. In The Alchemist, by Paolo Coelho, these stones are a gift to the protagonist to help him on his journey.

Bees: Bees are a symbol of industry and what can be done through cooperation. The bees foreshadow the split within the group as some move to the cave.

Caves: Entering caves for safety and slumber represents returning to the womb of mother earth. Caves are also archetypal symbols for the mind and sleep. Those that enter the caves may have the opportunity to be reborn or awakened.

Listen to What the Fans Say

Some fan wonder if some sort of time warp phenomenon is happening on the island. If so, is it possible that finding in

Adam and Eve, Jack and Kate are actually finding themselves laid to rest? Others wonder if it's merely foreshadowing, but again that ultimately Jack and Kate will find their final resting place in the cave.

Other fans have toyed with the idea that the two skeletons in the cave are aviator Amelia Earhart and her navigator Fred Noonan, who both vanished over the Pacific Ocean in 1937. Is it possible that the famous aviators were pulled into the island trap and ended their lives missing and lost?

Truth & Speculation

- There are no subtitles when Korean is spoken and others are present, only when Jin and Sun are alone.

- ABC played a commercial for the Oceanic website in conjunction with this episode

- The theory that Jin's watch is actually carrying an ultra-secret chip that was being manufactured by Sun's father for less than honorable purposes has been dispelled as not true by the creators.

Quotable Quips

- **Kate** (to Jack): Are you one of those hardcore spinal surgeons?

- **Charlie** (to Locke): It wouldn't be an irrational fear of bees if I could pull myself together would it?

- **Jack** (to Kate): We don't need to bring the water to the people. We need to bring the people to the water.

- **Sayid** (to Jack): Is there a reason why you didn't consult us when you decided to form your own civilization?

- **Locke** (to Charlie): What I know is that this island just might give you what you're looking for, but you have to give the island something.

Sawyerisms

- **To Kate:** Belle of the Ball

- **To Sayid:** Captain Falafel

- **To Sayid**: Omar

Seven Degrees of LOST

Jin is standing behind **Jack** in line at the airport.
Jin and **Sun** are married.
Locke is a fan of Drive Shaft and owns both their albums.

Episode Seven: The Moth

Summary

Charlie strums his guitar, but is obviously having a tough time with the withdrawals. Locke convinces him to come for a walk. Much to his chagrin, Charlie finds that Locke has actually lured him out into the jungle to be the bait for a successful boar trap. Charlie demands his drugs back. Locke refuses, telling him he's stronger than he thinks, that he needs to make the decision to quit on his own. However, if Charlie asks three times he will return the drug.

Jack continues to try to convince Kate to come to the caves, but she is determined to stay on the beach and assist Sayid with his plan of triangulating the French signal. Sayid is prepared to set up three antennae which if switched on at the same time should allow just enough time to locate the signal source. He has found some bottle rockets that can be used for signal flare to tell each person manning the antennae when to switch it on. However, he has no battery for the receiver. A laptop battery will probably work and Kate knows where to find one, Sawyer.

Charlie tries to help Jack move some suitcases, but only manages to make a mess. Jack notices that Charlie isn't looking well and also catches him looking for drugs to ease the withdrawals. Hurley hurts Charlie's feelings, telling him Jack wants his guitar case out of the way. All of this leads to Charlie confronting Jack in the caves about thinking he's worthless. Just as Charlie is yelling at him that he's a Rock God, a cave in starts. Charlie escapes, but Jack is trapped inside.

Everybody mobilizes to help Jack out of the cave. Hurley sends Charlie to the beach to get more help. Charlie finds Boone, who gives Shannon the responsibility of firing one of the signal flares and turning on the signal. Kate and Sayid are already on their way into the jungle and Sawyer goes to find them and let them know.

Sawyer finds Kate, but she has such a bad attitude with him that he doesn't tell her about Jack and says he's coming to help them instead. Sayid leaves Kate with Sawyer to mount the second antennae while Sayid takes the third. Sawyer, in a moment of spite, tells Kate that Jack has been buried in a cave in and Kate leaves him with the responsibility of the antennae, running to the caves.

Charlie finds Locke, but not to tell him about Jack. He wants his stash. He can't stand the way he's feeling. Locke shows him a cocoon and tells him a parable. He says that there's a moth inside trying to work its way out. Locke could take his knife and gently widen the opening to help the struggling moth, but then it would emerge too weak to survive. The struggle is nature's way of ensuring it emerges strong enough. Locke tells Charlie if he asks one more time for the drugs he will give them to him.

Michael inspects to the cave to figure out where they can dig out without causing further collapse. They create an opening, but Jack is pinned inside. Someone has to go in and help him. It's a small opening and as everyone is deliberating over who should go in, Charlie appears and volunteers. He points out that he is alone on the island, no sister, no wife, no child, no one depending on him.

Charlie wriggles through the tunnel and as he near the end it begins to collapse again. He barely gets into the chamber with Jack as the tunnel caves in. Charlie frees Jack, but Jack's shoulder is dislocated. Jack convinces him to pop it back into place. Charlie doesn't think he can do it, but manages. Jack asks how long he's had a fix and Charlie admits to being in withdrawal. Charlie berates himself, but Jack points out how much courage it took to come in and try to rescue him, although they are now both trapped.

Charlie suddenly notices a moth in the cave with them and then it disappears. He follows the moth to a small opening in the ceiling and begins to dig. While the others frantically try to dig through the cave in, Jack and Charlie appear, dirty, but no worse for wear. Charlie is a hero.

In the jungle, Sayid lights the first flare. Shannon lights hers as well, but nearly forgets. Sayid sees it and waits for the third flare. It too lights up the sky. The receiver in his hand is acquiring a signal when suddenly, someone swings a branch into Sayid's head and knocks him out.

The survivors gather around a fire at the cave. Kate makes Jack a sling. Walt asks his father if they can stay and live at the caves. Charlie gets up and goes for a walk to go find Locke who is roasting boar. Charlie asks for drugs back, but when Locke gives them to him, he throws them on the fire. As the fire burns the drugs to smoke an the smoke lifts into the sky, Charlie looks up and sees a moth flying away.

Charlie Pace 101

Charlie gives a sincere confession to a priest from his side of the booth, despite its hilarity. His confessions are about his indiscretions with groupies and how the opportunities have just arisen because of the local success of this band,

Drive Shaft. The priest points out that temptation are plenty but the test is to not give in to them. Charlie agrees, vowing to quit the band. The only problem is that Liam, his younger brother is waiting for him in the church with a recording contract. Liam promises that Charlie is going to be a rock god, after all, he's the songwriter. Liam is just a pretty face. Charlie however, worried about where this all might lead, makes Liam promise that if he says they're done, they walk away.

On stage the band is a success singing, "You All Everybody," but the fans are screaming for Liam. Caught up in it all, Liam sings Charlie's part of the song. Charlie is angry, but Liam doesn't see the problem.

Soon after Liam is really caught up; missing sound checks, doing drugs, and surrounding himself with willing female groupies. Charlie demands that he make good on his promise that if things get out of hand they quit. Liam won't hear it yelling that *he* is Drive Shaft and Charlie is nothing. Devastated, Charlie examines Liam's drug stash and cries.

On his way to get on Oceanic Flight #815, Charlie stops by his brother's house. Years have passed and Liam is off the drugs and raising a family. Charlie is in disarray and Liam chastises him for not returning his calls. Charlie is there with a motive though; he wants Liam to rejoin the band for a tour that starts in a Los Angeles, a tour that won't be booked without Liam fronting the band. Liam won't do it and is furious when it becomes apparent that Charlie is still a junkie. Charlie blames his brother for his own drug abuse and walks away, refusing any help.

Analyze This

Emerging from the tunnel: As Charlie squirms through the tunnel and into the opening where Jack is trapped, the imagery is that of squeezing through a birth canal or from a cocoon and into a new world. Symbolically Charlie is being reborn as a hero, coming to Jack's rescue.

Will Charlie utilize this new life or fall back into the trap of addiction?

Bottle-Rockets: The bottle rockets represent responsibility and dependability. Shannon and Sawyer are the two least dependable people on the island, yet they ultimately come through. Does this mean that we are meant to understand that there is more depth to the both of them?

Signs & Symbols

Charlie's Hood: Charlie's hood symbolizes his separation from the other survivors. He pulls his hood down, lowering his face and keeping others from "seeing" him. At the end of the episode when Charlie throws his hood back and looks up into the sky, he becomes a part of the group.

Drugs: The drugs that Charlie is addicted to symbolize the trappings and pitfalls of the world that Charlie must leave behind in order to survive on the island. Drugs are a way to escape from reality, but survival on the island will require full engagement.

Flying Moth: The moth represents freedom and hope. The moth has emerged from the cocoon strong and bound for the sky. Perhaps Charlie can do the same.

Listen to What the Fans Say

Could the island possibly be Atlantis? The island of Atlantis, if it existed, was thought to have sunk. It too was a tropical island with a strange power source. There is a theory that the island would rise up out of the ocean again. The Mayans too spoke of a lost island named Mu that is believed to be another telling of Atlantis. Is it possible that the survivors have found themselves on the mystical land of Atlantis, an island that is uncharted because it is rising from the ocean?

Truth & Speculation

- "You all Everybody" is an inside joke based on something that was said by a guest on the Phil Donahue Show

- Drive Shaft was originally called Petting Zoo in the script

- Charlie has proved so popular that the show's producers made an unusual public pledge that he will never be killed

Quotable Quips

- **Kate**: (to Jack about her mugshot): I take better pictures than that...Smaller too if you if you want something for your wallet.

- **Charlie** (to Jack): You don't' know me. I'm a bloody Rock God!

- **Kate** (to Sayid about the plane crash): Sorry, Sayid, but some things just happen—no rhyme, no reason.

- **Locke** (to Charlie about the moth): "Struggle is Nature's way of strengthening it."

- **Charlie** (to Jack): I'm, uh, ...I'm here to rescue you.

Sawyerisms

- **To Charlie:** Amigo

- **About Sayid**: Mohammad

- **To Sayid:** Boss

- **About Jack**: Jacko

- **To Kate**: Sweetheart

- **To Charlie**: Sport

- **About Jack**: Saint Jack

Seven Degrees of LOST

Locke is a fan of Drive Shaft, **Charlie**'s band
Charlie's shirt says St. Tropez which is where **Shannon** went to school in France

Episode Eight: Confidence Man

Summary

Jack cares for the wound on Sayid's head, but no one is sure who attacked him. Sayid accuses Locke, but Locke implicates Sawyer and gives Sayid a knife. Locke's argument is convincing and Sayid takes the weapon.

Sawyer has beat up Boone for going through his things. Shannon needs inhalers for her asthma and Boone is certain that Sawyer has them. Sawyer, after all, is reading Boone's book, *Watership Down*, which was in his suitcase with the inhalers. He must have the inhalers as well. Sawyer won't give the medicine to Jack and they almost get into a fight which Kate breaks up. Kate offers to try to talk to Sawyer herself.

Kate asks Sawyer what he wants for the inhalers. Sawyer wants a kiss. Kate balks and claims that she can see past his "act". She's seen the letter he reads and thinks he's more human than he lets on. Sawyer is incensed that she thinks she knows him and gives her the letter to read. The letter is from a little boy that says that Mr. Sawyer was responsible for killing his parents. Kate is shaken up by the letter.

When Shannon begins to have an asthma attack, Jack gives in to his anger and attacks Sawyer, but gets nowhere. Jack goes back to Shannon and is able to calm her and help her get the attack under control, but she's going to need her medicine. Sayid suggests that he convince Sawyer with the techniques he learned serving in The Republican Guard. Jack agrees.

Charlie tries to convince Claire to join the others at the caves. She's unconvinced that the caves are a better place for her to be. Talking about the things that they miss, Charlie discovers that Claire misses peanut butter more than any other food. He makes her promise that if he can get her some, she'll move to the caves. On a mission to find peanut butter Charlie approaches Hurley, thinking he'll make it from the little packets of peanuts the airline gives out, but all the food from the plane is gone.

Jack and Sayid find Sawyer sleeping and abduct him. Sayid tortures Sawyer, but still he won't give up the medicine. When Sayid threatens to cut Sawyer's face with the knife, Sawyer finally relents but will only tell Kate. The others bring Kate to him and she kisses him as per the previous bargain. It's then that Sawyer professes that he doesn't have the medicine and never did. Kate punches him.

Kate tells Sayid and Jack that he doesn't have the inhalers and Sayid loses it, sure he's lying. Sayid believes he destroyed the transceiver as well. He jumps Sawyer with the knife and plunges it into his right arm. The knife hits an artery and Jack jumps in to save Sawyer's life.

Sawyer rests in his tent and Kate shows up. She reread the letter and gave it more thought. The envelope is marked with America's Bicentennial. Knoxville, Tennessee. She knows that Sawyer wrote it and when he did he was only a kid. Sawyer admits this is true, that the real Sawyer was the confidence man that took advantage of his parents. He took his name and when he became a con man himself, became the man he was chasing.

Sun has been watching Shannon and gets Michael to help her gather eucalyptus. With the leaves she makes a mixture to put on Shannon's chest. It works like a charm. Shannon can breathe again.

Charlie, unsuccessful at finding or making peanut butter comes up with a more imaginative plan. He brings her an empty jar and together they imagine they are eating peanut butter, they best peanut butter either has ever tasted. Claire is charmed with the game.

Sayid in the mean time is grappling with what he has done to Sawyer. What he has done is something he had promised himself never to do again. The guilt is too much and he tells Kate he's leaving. Someone has to walk the shore and map the island. He leaves Kate standing on the beach.

Sawyer 101

Sawyer is late for a meeting because he has been preoccupied with a woman in his bed. As he rushes off to leave he "accidentally" spills the contents of his briefcase, $140,000 in bills. He tells the woman, Jessica that it's his life savings and he's investing it in an oil mining operation with another guy fifty/fifty. In a few weeks they'll be splitting a million dollars. Jessica wants in on the deal and thinks her husband will cough up the money.

Over lunch Sawyer tells the couple that perhaps this isn't such a good idea. He works with Jessica at the car dealership and business between friends can get sticky. Jessica insists, but her husband, David is a little uncertain. Sawyer offers him the cash he has to hold and see that the deal is serious. When David still seems reluctant, Sawyer gets up to walk out on the deal, but David calls him back.

Sawyer meets Kilo, the man who fronted the money in a pool hall. Kilo isn't so thrilled about the idea of having left the money with a "civilian." Sawyer is certain that it was the best way to seal the deal. Kilo points out that if he doesn't have his money back, plus fifty-percent by the next day, Sawyer is going to suffer.

At David and Jessica's house, he closes the deal. He's about to walk off with the money when their little boy gets up and asks his mother to read to him. Sawyer stares at the boy and then has a change of heart. He calls the deal off and drops both suitcases before he walks out the door.

Analyze This

Torture: In the end who tortured whom? Sawyer seems to want to be hated and injured. He seems to believe that he deserves every ounce of pain inflicted on him. When Sayid tortured him, Sayid was only torturing himself. The Iraqi forced himself to again experience a part of himself he wanted to extinguish. Perhaps there are repercussions for everything inflicted on another individual on this island.

Imaginary Peanut Butter: Food is a common theme on the island. Food is both sustenance and deprivation. Perhaps by offering Claire imagery peanut butter and forcing her to use her imagination to indulge in it, Charlie has taught Claire the value her own mind. Food is a necessity, but the extras really only have value in the way you perceive them.

Signs & Symbols

Anger: Anyone who loses control of their anger is in danger of losing control entirely. By provoking anger, Sawyer is able to get Jake, Sayid, and even Kate to do things they would not normally do.

Kiss: Bartering for a kiss is all about control and even violation. Kissing may also be used to signify reverence and subordination, as in kissing the ring of a king or pope. A kiss can also be rude or done for the sake of proving one's superiority.

Asthma: The inability to breathe symbolizes the realization of lack of control. Shannon, who has been completely in denial up until this point, must now deal with the obvious. The survivors may not be rescued. Shannon is not totally in control of her own future.

Inhalers: Like Charlie's drugs, the inhalers that Shannon depends on are another symbol of the trappings of a modern world that can no longer be depended on if the remaining passengers of flight 815 are to survive.

Listen to What the Fans Say

Is it possible that the plane flew through a rip in the space/time continuum? Perhaps the survivors aren't on earth at all, but in an alternate reality. Proponents of this theory note that the plane dropped from 40,000 feet but didn't break up until it was a few thousand feet from the ground, that the island is uncharted, that sixteen years worth of transmissions were somehow never heard by the outside world. And of course, there is the small fact of a polar bear on a tropical island.

Truth & Speculation

- Josh Holloway spent eight years trying to break into acting. He had gotten his real estate license and was ready to quit when he was asked to join the LOST cast.

- James Garner recently pointed at Josh Holloway and said, "That kid has a shot."

- Once Holloway was awarded the role of Sawyer he felt he could support his long time girlfriend, Yessica and proposed.

Quotable Quips

- **Boone** (regarding Shannon using her inhaler) She's just been embarrassed about it since she was a little kid. I guess breathing's not cool.

- **Sawyer:** (to Jack) Look, I don't know what kind of commie share-fest you're running over in cave-town, but down here possession's nine-tenths of the law.

- **Hurley** (to Jack): Wow, man. That was awesome. I mean, that was like a... Jedi moment.

- **Hurley** (to Charlie): I'm a big guy, it's going to be a while before you're going to want to give me a piggy back ride, okay?

- **Sawyer** (to Kate): Baby, I am tied to a tree in a jungle of mystery. I just got tortured by a damn spinal surgeon and a genuine Iraqi.

Sawyerisms

- **To Sayid:** Ali
- **To Kate:** Freckles
- **To Jack:** Chico
- **To Kate:** Baby
- **To Jack:** Cowboy
- **To Boone:** Son

Seven Degrees of LOST

Sawyer is actually the name of the man that killed "Sawyer's parents.

Episode Nine: Solitary

Summary

Carrying a photograph of a woman with Arabic writing on the back, Sayid is scouting the shore. He finds a cable half buried in the sand. Intrigued, he follows it into the jungle. He finds a trip line in the plants, clearing it successfully, but still he sets off another trap. Netted and hanging by his ankles, Sayid is trapped until after sundown. When at last someone comes and cuts him down, he passes out before he can see who it is.

When Sayid comes to, he can hear a woman asking in several languages, "Where's Alex." His vision clears to reveal a middle-aged woman and when he has no answer for her, she shocks him by running electricity through the old wire bed frame on which he is tied. When he still doesn't have an answer, the woman shocks him again.

Sayid tries to explain that he is a plane crash survivor and he followed the cable from the beach. He was only trying to discover from where the mayday transmission was being

sent. He says it was on a loop for sixteen years. The woman is

little surprised in the time that has passed. It was here signal.

She doesn't believe Sayid's intentions however and knocks

him out.

When Sayid awakes, the woman has discovered Sayid's

photos of Nadia. She wants to know who she is and what is

written on the back of the photo, but Sayid won't tell her

unless he knows who Alex is. The woman, who he now

knows as Rousseau from reading the name a jacket, won't

tell him a thing. Sayid offers to fix a music box that is

obviously dear to her and she injects him with something

that again knocks him out.

When Sayid wakes this time, he is chained to a table, the

music box in front of him. The woman reveals that her name

is Danielle Rousseau and that she was a part of a science

team whose ship ran aground on the island. She mentions

the Black Rock, the Others and that she team got sick. She

claims to hear the Others out in the jungle. When he doesn't get anything else out of her, he fixes the music box and asks her to set him free. She refuses. When she leaves to address a noise outside Sayid frees himself and grabs a rifle he finds.

In the jungle he encounters Danielle who also carries a gun but neither is willing to lower their weapon. When Sayid pulls the trigger he finds that the rifle doesn't fire. Danielle has removed the firing pin, something she did before she shot her husband, Robert who had the sickness. Sayid asserts that he isn't sick. He tells her that the writing on the back of Nadia's photograph says, "You will find me in the next life, if not his one." He points out that she doesn't have to be alone that the help of friends could help them get off the island. She lets him go, telling him that Alex was her child, but disappears into the forest.

Jack treats a man named Sullivan for hives who like the rest of the survivors seems a little stir crazy. When Jack tells the man to try to keep his mind off it, Hurley points out to him that there is really nothing else to think about on the island, no diversions. Jack is not interested in his thoughts.

Locke has been hunting with Ethan, a man who according to Locke is a capable tracker. They have found some suitcases in the jungle and bring them to Hurley to look through. Walt approaches Locke wanting to learn how to hunt, but his father puts a quick stop to it.

Hurley unearths all of the necessities of golf in various suitcases and has set up a two-hole course. He has Charley go get Jack to take a look at it. Hurley convinces Jack that what they need more than anything is a diversion and Michael, Charlie, Hurley and Jack begin a game. It isn't long before others join them. Soon everyone is relaxed. Michael has forgotten about Walt though. Walt arrives, upset that his father has left him alone and when Michael is still preoccupied with the game, Walt runs off to find Locke.

While the other survivors, even Sawyer, are playfully betting on the golf game, Walt has asked Locke to teach him to throw a knife. Elsewhere, Sayid is making his way back to the survivors. Somewhere in the jungle he encounters an unfamiliar sound. Sayid hears the sound of people whispering all around him.

Sayid 101

In an interrogation room in Iraq Sayid beats a prisoner. Sayid is accusing him of planting a bomb and killing two soldiers and is trying to torture the truth out of him. Omar, Sayid's superior watches and when the leave expresses his approval of the way Sayid handled himself. Omar has put in for Sayid's reassignment to the intelligence division and a promotion. Sayid is pleased, but distracted for a moment when a female prisoner is escorted by him in the hall.

The woman is Noor Abed Jazeem and she is connected to Kurdish and Shiite insurgents. Sayid is instructed to find out if she knows who orchestrated the bombings. When he goes in to interrogate her, he finds that she is a childhood friend, a girl he knew as Nadia. Still he is determined to get the information from her. Nadia is unfazed. She has been tortured by the Republican Guard before.

Several weeks later Nadia is still in the cell. Sayid brings her some bread and promises to try to bring more later. He asks her to identify some photos. He's certain he can get her released if she seems cooperative. She jokes that were she released that she wouldn't have his visits to look forward to anymore. Sayid snaps that it's not game and Nadia points out that he is the one playing it.

In light of the fact that Nadia has given them no useful information, Omar instructs Sayid to execute her. Sayid asks for more time, but Omar feels her death will send a message to others that are uncooperative. There is no swaying him.

Sayid escorts Nadia out as if to be executed, but excuses the guards walking with him at an opportune moment. Sayid frees Nadia and explains to Nadia how to escape. She asks him to come, but he can't risk desertion. She takes a photo that was on her file and a pen from Sayid's pocket and writes something on the back. Omar appears and asks what is happening. As he calls the guard, Sayid shoots him before he can raise further alarm. To cover for the incident he shoots himself in the leg and hands the gun to Nadia. He will pretend like she has shot them both and escaped, but she must run. Nadia grabs the gun and escapes.

Analyze This

Solitary: The title is also the overall theme of this episode is about the dangers of remaining solitary in the struggle for survival. As Sayid tells Danielle, they are all more likely to get off the island if they work together. The ghosts of the past shouldn't be allowed to get in the way of the needs of the present. This realization is echoed when Sawyer participates in the betting on the golf course. At last Sawyer makes an effort to join the crowd. Will the lesson be a permanent one or will the survivors continue to allow themselves to be splintered?

Prisoner: The symbolism of who is and is not a prisoner is critical to this episode. Those who do not let their mind become imprisoned, like Nadia and ultimately Sayid when captured by Danielle, remain free. Sayid was actually the prisoner while Nadia was his captive. He was a slave to the ideals and fallacies of The Republican Guard. Danielle is a prisoner of the island and her past while she is the captor of Sayid. Both need to learn that physical chains are not what makes one a captive. Sayid seems to have discovered this, but will Danielle?

Signs & Symbols

Music box: The music box like some many other tangible items the survivors cling to, symbolizes the trappings of a modern world and the inability to release them. Danielle has suffered alone for a long time because of her determination to cling to the music box.

Sickness: sickness could be physical ailments brought on by living on the island, but it could also symbolize what happens to those who give up and can no longer mentally survive.

Golf: The game of golf symbolizes the ability to work together and still be competitive. This is the first instance of the survivors creating a new form of civility to ease their stay on the island.

The Others: The others symbolize another aspect of the unknown on the island. Even their whispers are unintelligible, both foreboding and unrevealing. Even now they remain a mystery.

Listen to What the Fans Say

Is it possible that the Island is like some sort of siren, drawing people in and giving everyone whatever they need, or think they need in order to want to stay? Some of the emotional needs of the survivors are fulfilled in simple ways. Kate is free at last of the law breathing down her neck. Other lures to integrating and enjoying this new society are obviously strange gifts doled out from something unknown.

Locke has back his mobility and the means to fulfill his dreams of becoming an effective strategist and capable hunter, for example. In later shows we find other reasons for characters to wish to remain on the island. Still the need to return to society will never diminish. Will the island continue to conjure up reasons for the survivors to stay put?

Truth & Speculation

- When asked by a reporter what he thought the "monster" might be, Naveen jokingly stated he and the cast wonder if perhaps it's a device the producers invented to rid themselves of unruly actors.

- Naveen had an affair with his high school teacher and has one child, a son, with her.

- Shannon's translation of the French woman's transmission is not quite correct. Here's what's really being said: *If anybody can hear this, they are dead. I'll try to go to the Black Rock. Please help us. He (or it) is outside, he's (it's) outside, and Brandon took the keys. Please help us. They are dead. They are all dead.*

Quotable Quips

- **Hurley** (to Jack): Our lives suck. Everyone's nerves are stretched to the max. I mean, we're lost on an island running from boars and monsters...freakin' polar bears!

- **Jack** (to Kate): I've been going crazy trying to make everyone feel safe. I haven't been sleeping because I want everyone to feel safe. He builds a golf course... and everyone feels safe.

- **Sawyer** (to Kate): A doctor playing golf. Whew! boy howdy, now I've heard everything. What's next? Cop eating a donut?

- **Sayid** (to Danielle about what's written on the photo) You'll find me in the next life, if not this one.

- **Sayid** (to Danielle) ...the more I hold on, the more I pull away from those around me. The only way off this...this place is with their help.

Sawyerisms
- **To Jack:** Jackass

- **To Jack:** Dr. Quinn

Seven Degrees of LOST
Nadia is the lost love of **Sayid** and the woman in the photo.
Danielle Rousseau is the voice of the transmission.

Episode Ten: Raised by Another

Summary

Claire wakes with a strange nightmare about her baby. In her dream Locke tells her that the baby was her responsibility but she has given him away, because of this everyone pays the price. When Claire goes to look for her baby all she finds is a puddle blood and she wakes screaming. Charlie tries to calm her down, but it takes him a while.

Jack checks Claire and asks her a bunch of questions. She's only a couple of weeks before her due date and up until now hasn't had any problems. Jack is worried, but doesn't let it show to anyone but Kate.

Charlie looks after Claire, teasing her and trying to get her to drink some tea. She seems less worried over her dream, but when she goes back to sleep that night she has another incident. This time she is certain that someone attacked her.

Charlie is determined to mobilize everyone and find the attacker.

No one finds Claire's assailant, but it occurs to Hurley that there's no census of who is who or where on the island. Hurley begins to quiz everyone the next day. He gets the manifest from the plane from Sawyer and double-checks against it. No one is thrilled about giving the information, but Hurley finesses it out of everyone the best he can.

Jack in the meantime is uncertain that Claire was even attacked. He thinks she is having anxiety dreams and that the pregnancy is intensifying them. Charlie is incensed. Jack ignores him. After all, his main concern is that Claire's stress levels might induce her labor at anytime. He tries to talk to her and give her a mild sedative, but Claire is furious and leaves the caves for the beach.

Charlie catches up with her halfway into the jungle. He tries to calm her down and talk some sense into her. She isn't even willing to let him help with her bags. Then she begins to have contractions. Claire demands that Charlie go get Jack.

Charlie runs back, but runs into Ethan on the path back to the caves. He asks him to go get the doctor and returns to Claire.

While their waiting, Claire tells Charlie the story of Richard Malkin's predictions. She explains why she was on this particular flight. As they discuss it she comes to a realization, there is no couple in Los Angeles waiting for her baby. Richard set her up.

Meanwhile, Sayid is hurrying through the jungle, making his way to Jack. When he gets there he explains that he found the French woman and that they are not alone. Hurley too has realized they're not alone. There is someone not on the manifest, someone who wasn't on the plane, Ethan Rom.

It's been a while and Jack still hasn't arrived, but Claire feels better and the contractions have stopped. They were probably false labor. She and Charlie get up and head back to the caves when Ethan appears. He doesn't say anything more than hello, but his expression is promises trouble.

Claire Littleton 101

Claire takes a pregnancy test and tells her boyfriend, Thomas that she is pregnant. Claire is uncertain what to do, but Thomas wants to have the baby and tells her that he loves her.

Two days later, Claire and her friend Rachel got to see a psychic, Richard Malkin. Richard reads Claire's hands and sees that she's pregnant. As he seems to be looking further, he gets worried then says he can't do the reading. He gives Claire back her money and insists that she leaves.

Claire moves in with Thomas, but three months later it's not working. This is a surprise to Claire, but Thomas seems to think there's suddenly too much responsibility in their lives. Claire tells him that he can't change his mind, but it's too late he has. Thomas leaves her.

Claire goes back to see the psychic a week later. She convinces him to do another reading and immediately sees that her boyfriend has left her. Then Richard tells her that

116

she has to raise the baby and no one else, otherwise the baby is in danger. Claire refuses, she is going to give the baby up for adoption. She runs out, shaken.

Months later, Richard is still calling her, begging her to reconsider and keep the baby. He isn't getting anywhere with her. She meets with an attorney and the potential parents of her unborn child. When she goes to sign the papers, twice the pen she is given doesn't work. She can't take it and doesn't sign the papers. Despite the protests in the room, she leaves.

Meeting with Richard Malkin, Claire is offered another deal. He says he's found a couple in Los Angeles who want the baby and he swears the baby will be safe with them. She gets $12,000 for the deal, but she has to leave on flight 815 the next day.

Analyze This

Claire's Nightmare: Locke in Claire's dream has black and white stones where his eyes should be. The stones, a sign of good and evil, right and wrong decisions, are a recurring symbol on the island. Does the dream indicate that Claire thinks she made the wrong decision by getting on the plane? Is there guilt that she may be responsible for the plane crashing or for the future of the world somehow because of her baby? The blood on her hands seems to be symbolic of guilt at the end of the dream. Or maybe the dream just foreshadows the ultimate fight for the baby.

A ticket to paradise: Why did Richard Malkin put Claire on Oceanic Flight 815? If he did it to keep the baby from being raised by another, does this mean he knew Claire would survive to raise her baby? Or did the possibility of the future look so bleak that he felt he had to doom Claire to death rather than let the baby live with someone else? If he was psychic enough to see this as the best solution, then perhaps we can feel assured that Claire and her baby will remain safe. Then again, some of the worst mistakes in history have been done with the hopes of heading off disaster. Perhaps Richard will ultimately hold the responsibility for separating mother and baby.

Signs & Symbols

Three times a charm: Claire is given three chances to make the right decision (he pen doesn't work the first two times she tries to sign) Just like Charlie get three chances to ask for his drugs. The number three is considered a powerful and holy number in many cultures.

Dream of losing teeth: Charlie tells Claire he dreams that he is losing his teeth. This sort of dream is often about a fear of how others view your outwardly appearance. No surprise that Charlie, frequently hidden beneath his hood would dream of this.

Sleepwalking: Sleepwalking is often symbolic of someone who is burdened with guilt, such as in Lady Macbeth's sleepwalking in Macbeth.

Listen to What the Fans Say

Could the island actually be some sort of prison or form of psychotherapy? Many fans have noted the variety of damaged goods in human packages that have arrived with the fallen plane. Survivors are guilt-ridden, self-center, delusional, even possibly sociopathic. What if the island is a virtual reality that puts everyone through the paces necessary to become whole, healed or functioning members of society? That might explain the strange occurrences and the amazing interlocking of all of their lives.

Truth & Speculation
- Ethan Rom is an anagram for "Other Man"

- The necklace that Claire wears is the Chinese symbol for love

- Thomas accuses Claire of having 'daddy issues." According to the writers "broken families" is one of the many themes of LOST

Quotable Quips

- **Charlie** (mimicking Claire writing in her diary): Dear Diary, Still on the bloody island. Today I swallowed a bug. Love Claire.

- **Charlie** (To Claire) Here. What separates us from these savage yanks if we can't drink tea?

- **Locke** (To Hurley's question, "Did you find it?"): No it found me.

- **Hurley** (to Ethan) Right on. Love Canada. Great, uh.... well that should do it. Thanks for your time dude.

- **Richard Malkin** (To Claire) Your nature, your spirit, your goodness must be an influence in the development of this child.

Sawyerisms

To Hurley: Stay-Puft

Seven Degrees of LOST

Claire is on the island because **Richard Malkin** tricked her and bought her a ticket.

Episode Eleven: All the Best Cowboys Have Daddy Issues

Summary

As soon as the survivors discover that Ethan isn't one them, they race off to find Charlie and Claire. Locke finds Claire's bag and signs of a struggle. Both Charlie and Claire seem to have been taken. It seems unlikely that Ethan could have drug both of them off, but Locke is more concerned with the "why?" He wants to organize a search party, but Jack immediately runs off to find them.

Locke goes back to the caves to get his knives and mobilize the troops. Kate and Boone ask to join him and Locke agrees, but won't let Michael come along when asks. Michael will have to take his own search party south in the opposite direction.

It doesn't take Locke long to catch up to Jack, who's been walking in a circle. Locke tries to talk him into going back to the camp, but Jack is staying. As they move further along he reveals to Kate that he thinks Claire's kidnapping was his fault, that he should have listened to her. Locke ends their conversation by yelling out to Jack. He's found on of the pieces of tape that Charlie wrapped around his fingers. The only problem is that now their trail is split and leading in two directions. Locke and Boone follow one while Jack and Kate follow the other.

Kate isn't as good at tracking as Locke, but they find another piece of tape from Charlie's fingers. Then Jack hears Claire screaming and knows their on the right trail. He runs off in the direction of the sound without waiting for Kate. Jack slips and falls, opening his eyes to find Ethan looking down on him. Ethan threatens to kill one of his captors if Jack doesn't stop following. Jack starts a fight instead of heeding the warning and promptly gets knocked out by Ethan.

Sawyer discovers that Sayid is back and pays him a visit. Sawyer offers Sayid veiled threats, but doesn't faze the Iraqi. Sayid tells him to go ahead and take a shot at him. He left the camp out of shame for what he had done to Sawyer. Then he tells Sawyer what happened to him in the jungle while he was gone. Sawyer tells him that the seemly unnatural tide has almost washed away the plane debris, but that he kept the signal fire burning for him.

When Jack comes to, Jack is with him but she hasn't seen Ethan. Jack still isn't convinced by the man's warning. He gets up in runs in the direction he think Ethan headed. Further in the jungle he and Kate come Charlie, but he's lifeless and hanging from a tree, a rope around his neck. Kate climbs up and cuts him down. Jack tries to resuscitate him, but he's not breathing. CPR is working and Kate is sobbing at Jack's side. She' given up, but Jack hasn't. He pounds on Charlie's chest again and again and suddenly Charlie gasps for air. Jack has saved him, but back at camp Charlie can't remember anything about the ordeal.

Locke and Boone have lost the trail; Locke is simply following his gut. He tries to convince Boone to go back, but Boone won't go. Further in though, Boone starts to worry that they're lost. He doesn't believe that Locke knows where he's going. Locke tosses him a flashlight to help him find his way back. When Boone fumbles the catch, the flashlight falls to the grounds making the clanking noise of hitting metal. Investigating they find it's a steel plate and begin to clear the earth off the top of it.

Jack Shephard 101

Jack is working on a patient in the operating room and she isn't doing well. She flatlines and jack tries to bring her back. He won't give up, but has no success. Another doctor stands in the room watching. He pulls down his mask to reveal that he's Christian, Jack's father. He tells Jack that it's over, to call it. Jack refuses and tells him to call it.

Jack's father is furious because Jack was upstairs, but barged in and took over the operation. Jack had a reason though. A nurse came and told him that his father was operating under the influence of alcohol. Christian is responsible for her death.

126

Later, Christian asks Jack to sign a statement of what happened. When Jack asks what it says, his father replies, "the truth." The woman came in suffering from massive internal bleeding due to a car crash and they were unable to save her life. Jack refuses to sign it even though he father tells him that if alcohol is mentioned he will lose his license. It isn't until Jack's father admits that he's been hard on him, that he's sacrificed bits of their relationship and that what happened with the patient won't happen again that Jack signs the statement.

The husband of the woman is suing and Christian gives an official version of what happened during an inquiry. Jack listens, but says nothing. As the inquiry wraps up Christian is asked if he was aware of the woman's pregnancy. Christian was in fact aware, but Jack had no idea. Jack speaks up and tells the truth, his father was intoxicated and cut the woman's hepatic artery, ultimately leading to her death.

Analyze This

Walt's seemingly strange powers: Walt seems to know that Sawyer is using an alias, alluding to it when he mentions that lying about your name is stupid. Walt also perfectly articulates what has happened with Ethan, Claire and Charlie as though he is entirely familiar, even more so than the adults, with all that is happening on the island. He's ability to win backgammon with lucky rolls over and over is also suspicious. Locke seems drawn to the boy as if he senses there is more to him than meets the eye. Is Walt somehow responsible for the happenings on the island?

Locke's weather prediction ability: It may not take a genius to guess it's going to rain on a tropical island, but Locke is able to pinpoint the exact moment it is about to rain. Is Locke somehow incredibly intuitive? Or is this another hint to his symbiotic relationship with the island?

Signs & Symbols

Pride: Pride is a common fatal flaw of the fallen hero, like Lucifer in Milton's *Paradise Lost* or Shakespeare's *Othello*,

Jack's father lets his pride get in the way of what is moral and falls beyond redemption.

Greater Good: Jack's father states that raising Jack with a heavy hand has been for the "greater good." This statement illuminates Jack's motives. Jack is always striving for the greater good without looking at the

Signal Fire: Sawyer kept the signal fire burning during Sayid's absence, an act that may signify respect from a man that seems to have little desire to go back to civilization. This act demonstrates that Sawyer understands that in many ways he and Sayid are kindred spirits.

Listen to What the Fans Say

Another speculation is that LOST is a game for the bored and wealthy. Perhaps some of the survivors are actors and others are unwitting participants, entertaining rich men who

smoke cigars and bet on each individual's outcome.
Otherwise how would you account for the strategic
placement of a doctor, a self-taught electrician, a
construction engineer, two trackers and a hunter? Could it
all be a carefully constructed game?

Truth & Speculation

- Damon Lindelof states that you can see everything about Locke's character in his first speaking scene with the backgammon set.

- Some of the that didn't know about the production of LOST thought there was a real plane crash and called to report it.

- There are overall themes to the show but individual writers bring their own thematic material to each episode

Quotable Quips

- **Locke** (to Jack): So go back, be the doctor. Let me be the hunter.

- **Michael** (to Hurley): All I'm saying is I'm getting sick of being treated like a second class citizen around her because Mount Baldy can bag a boar.

- **Hurley** (to Walt): Back home I'm known as something of a warrior myself.

- **Sawyer** (to Walt) So a tribe of evil natives planted a ringer in the camp to kidnap a pregnant girl and a reject from VH-1 has-beens. Yeah, fiendishly clever. And why am I getting the evening news from a six year old?

- **Boone** (Guessing what Locke does for a living): Well, You're either a taxidermist or a hit man.

Sawyerisms

- **About Charlie**: Reject from VH-1 Has-Beens
- **About Jack**: Doctor Do-Right
- **To Walt**: Tattoo

Seven Degrees of LOST

Boone runs one of the subsidiaries of his mother's wedding business.

Jack is responsible for his father running off to Australia.

Locke is the regional collection manager for a box company.

Episode Twelve: Whatever the Case May Be

Summary

Sawyer trails Kate while she gathers fruit deeper in the jungle than normal. Kate notices she is being followed and throws a rock in the direction she hears a noise. She manages to hit Sawyer in the knee, who swears he was only protecting her. She notices the sound of falling water and leads him in the direction of the noise. They find an inviting waterfall and crystal clear pool.

In need of some relaxation, they both jump in to swim and play. Diving in from the rocks, they swim deeper and find a surprise at the bottom. There are two bodies, a man and woman still fastened to their airline seats in the pond.

They surface and Sawyer goes back to check what they have on them. Kate follows and sees a silver briefcase under the seats while Sawyer finds a wallet. Back at the surface Kate asks Sawyer to help with the briefcase and they go back and retrieve it. The case, however, is locked. Sawyer, realizing it's not Kate's decides he should take it. Kate feigns indifference, but it's obvious she wants it for some reason.

Kate tries to steal the suitcase from Sawyer, but with no luck. Now Sawyer is certain the case is meaningful to her and is even more determined to figure out how to open it. The problem is that it's a Halliburton, a case that is practically impossible to break into. When he tries opening it by dropping it from a cliff, Kate steals it again, but not for long. Sawyer overpowers her and takes it away. He'll give it to her if she just tells him what's inside, but she refuses.

On the beach the remainder of the wreckage is being washed out to sea by a strange shift and rise of the tides. Jack tries to convince Sayid again to lead those camped on the beach to the caves. After Claire's kidnapping Sayid is certain that would be a hard sell. Jack suggests they find Rousseau and the answer to who might have kidnapped Claire. Sayid doesn't think that's a good idea either. Jack proposes a harder look at the papers Sayid took from her.

There is something written in French on the papers and Sayid takes them to Shannon. She doesn't think she can help him, but after being told that she useless by her brother is easily convinces to give it a try. She has trouble and gets frustrated, but eventually realizes that the French writing is lyrics to a song called "La Mer."

Kate goes to Jack to try and get her help with the case. She reveals to him that it was the Marshal's case, holding four 9mm guns, ammo and some of his personal stuff. She tells him that Sawyer has the case and they agree it would be best if he didn't figure out how to open it and get to the guns. Kate knows where the key is, it's in the Marshal's wallet in his back pocket. She needs to know where he was buried.

Jack wants to know what else is in the case, but Kate says that there's nothing else. He demands the truth and she swears that is the truth. Jack agrees to help her, but only if they open the case together. They dig up the Marshal's body, but Kate pulls the key out of the wallet with a sleight of hand move. Jack catches it though and takes the key from her, disappointed.

Jack gets the case from Sawyer by threatening to stop his antibiotics. He takes the case to Kate despite her deception. The agreement was to open it together and they do. Inside he finds what Kate described as well as a letter-sized envelope. He hands it to Kate, asking if the envelope was what she wanted. Kate opens it, revealing a toy airplane. When Jack presses her for the importance of the toy she tells him it belonged to the man she loved. When Jack doesn't believe her she says it belonged to the man she killed.

Locke and Boone continue to go into the jungle to work on opening the hatch while claiming to be hunting and looking for Claire. Charlie meanwhile, pines away on the beach for Claire, blaming himself. He is approached by Rose who convinces him he did he best to save her. He needs to ask for help. Together Rose and Charlie pray.

Kate Austen/ Maggie Ryan 101

Kate poses as a photographer named "Maggie Ryan" at a bank in New Mexico where she fills out a loan application. She is making small talk with the manager Mark Hutton when armed robbers bust into the bank. The robbers send hustle the customers, including Kate and tellers to the floor and focus on the manager. They want the money cage opened.

Mark Hutton won't give up the key, believing he'll get killed either way. While the robber try to convince him, a trucker next to Kate tells her he thinks he can take them. The trucker manages to wrestle a gun away from one of the robbers and it falls, sliding over to Kate. The trucker yells at Kate to pick it up, but she won't shoot it. She claims she doesn't know how to use it.

Jason, one of the robbers, takes it away from her and drags her into another room to talk. Alone he pulls off his mask and laughs, telling her it was brilliant to pretend to be inept with a gun and they kiss. At Kate's insistence and in order to convince Mark Hutton that she is in danger, Jason hits her and cuts her lip.

The sight of Kate and her feigned fear, Mark Hutton agrees to open the vault. Inside the vault, Mark begs for Kate to be let go. Jason laughs and spills the beans; Kate was in on it. Then he does something Kate doesn't expect, he takes off his mask and prepares to shoot Mark. No on was supposed to get hurt, and Kate springs into action grabbing one of the other robber's guns.

Kate threatens Jason and when he doesn't believe her, she shoots him in the leg and one of the other gunmen in the arm. Kate asks Mark for the key to safety deposit box 815. She has the customer key but isn't on the signatory card. Inside the box is a letter sized envelope with something inside.

Analyze This

Truth: Revealing and hiding the truth is an important theme in LOST. In last episode Jack asks Kate for a little honesty and again in this episode. When Kate does tell the truth it's painful, but she at last cries with release. The truth after all can set you free and perhaps even help you get off the island.

Keys: This episode revolves around multiple keys; the key to the vault, the key to safety deposit box 815 and the key to the Halliburton. Having a key gives Kate access and ownership to the thing that she wants. However, the key isn't easily retrieved. The key requires truth, honesty and even confession. They key stands for the things that Kate has done and owning the key will allow her to make amends for them, but will she?

Signs & Symbols

Rising Tide: The tide is yet another reminder of the whims of the island and the survivors' lack of control when it comes to their environment. Only the moon controls the tides and its pull on this island is unpredictable.

Toy Airplane: The toy airplane is the symbol of the world outside the island the Kate must make amends with and let go of, just like Charlie's drugs and Locke's wheelchair.

Praying: Charlie reaches a place in his lack of faith where he must turn to the God he originally trusted to move on. Rose praying with symbolizes his turn back to originally pure path and foreshadows his relationship God in future episodes.

Listen to What the Fans Say

Is it possible that the island and everything on it is created by the minds of the survivors? Perhaps some force is tapping into the minds of those that survived flight 815 and making their wishes and fears come true. Supporters of this argument point to episodes of Star Trek, and the movies Sphere and Solaris to demonstrate this storyline in other science fiction. It is possible that this is due to aliens, a scientific experiement or perhaps just one person on the plane who had the ability to help everyone project. (Walt?)

140

Or perhaps just the collective desire of so many people to not get to their destination (Kate, Locke, Walt, Sawyer, etc) caused the plane to crash.

Truth & Speculation

- It's said that the rising tide was added to the story line as a device to remove the wreckage set from the beach in Hawaii.

- Evangeline Lilly and Dominic Monaghan met on the set of LOST and are now linked romantically

- Jorge Garcia offered Evangeline $20 to pee in a garbage can Kailua and had to pay her.

Quotable Quips

- **Sawyer** (to Kate): Oh of course, "I don't need protecting. I can take care of myself. Me Kate. Me throw rock"

- **Jack** (to Sayid about the tide): There's a lot not normal around here.

- **Sawyer** (to Kate): Gosh, I hate to bicker about positions, sweetheart, but I think you're the one on top.

- **Michael** (to Sawyer): If you pick the lock on a Halliburton, I'll put you on my back and fly us to L.A.

- **Shannon** (to Sayid): Do you ever think that after sixteen years on mystery frickin' island, your friend might not be quite adjusted.

Sawyerisms

To Kate: Freckles

To Michael: Daddy

To Jack: Brother

Seven Degrees of LOST

Shannon knows the lyrics to "La Mer" which **Rousseau** wrote on the her papers

Episode Thirteen: Hearts and Minds

Summary

Boone is unhappy with the way Sayid and Shannon's relationship is developing. He confronts Sayid, but doesn't seem to get anywhere with him. Locke tells Boone that he needs to lay off, that they'll need Sayid.

Hurley is concerned that Boone and Locke aren't coming back with any boar. He's having digestion problems. When he approaches Jack about this problem, Jack suggests he eat more protein and that Jin is catching plenty of fish. Hurley is certain that Jin has had a vendetta against him every since he turned down the offer of sea urchin. However, Jin is his only option for help getting meat.

In the jungle Locke and Boone continue to try to figure out how to open the hatch. With no handle, latch or other way of opening it has become a quandary. Boone warns Locke that the others are starting to worry about them not coming back with boar. He wants to tell Shannon the truth of what they are doing. Locke wonders if Boone is certain that this is what he wants to do and when Boone replies that he is certain, Locke knocks him out.

Boone wakes tied to a tree and Locke smears some sort of paste on his head wound. Locke throw a knife into the ground just out of Boone's reach and leaves. Boone tries to reach the knife, but the ropes are too painful.

When Boone hears Shannon screaming that she's tied up too and hears the "monster" coming, he gets the motivation he needs and reaches the knife. He cuts himself loose, finds Shannon and cuts her loose and the two of them flee the monster. They hide inside a thicket of trees and the monster pounds on the outside trying to get to them. When the monster leaves, they make their way through the jungle trying to figure out why Locke did this. It isn't long before the monster appears again. This time it gets Shannon and she doesn't survive.

Hurley approaches Jin and tries to communicate that he wants to know where to get fish. Jin seems more amused than helpful, but Hurley follows him out and tries to catch his own fish with a poor excuse of a self-made net. He doesn't have luck and worse steps on an urchin. Jin helps him and gives him some to eat. Hurley doesn't refuse this time, but vomits when he eats it. Later Jin brings Hurley a fish.

Jack finds Kate gathering seeds in the jungle and she shows him the garden that Sun is cultivating. Kate has been working with her in the garden and has discovered that she speaks English, but promises to tell no one. In the meantime Sayid discovers that compasses don't work correctly, yet another anomaly of the island. Yet gardening seems to be a bit of normalcy and Jack brings Kate the gift of some guava seeds.

Boone is devastated by the death of his sister and attacks Locke as soon as he finds him. Locke calms him down and asks why there is no blood on his shirt if he held his sister while she died. A little further away at the camp, Shannon's voice rises and there's no doubt that she's is alive. Locke explains that he drugged him and Boone understands why when he realizes that what he felt more than anything about Shannon's demise was relief. The two rise and walk into the jungle.

Boone & Shannon 101

Boone get a call from Shannon that leads him to believe she is in trouble and he races off to Sydney to save her. When he arrives, he finds her living with Bryan and although she says she's fine, she strategically reveals a bruise on her forehead. Boone leaves, but heads directly for the police station.

The police say that they can't do anything for him. Boone doesn't have any real evidence and isn't even a blood relative. He's Shannon's step-brother. So Boone goes to the docks where Bryan is and offers to pay him off. He ends up writing the man a check for $50,000.

Boone goes back to pick up Shannon and finds Bryan still at the house. Shannon won't leave and Bryan reveal to Boone that he's been set up. Shannon thinks she deserves the money because Boone's mother took it all when her father died. Bryan and Boone get in a fistfight, Shannon breaks it up and Boone leaves.

That night Shannon shows up at Boone's hotel room. She tells him that she's been played, Bryan took the money. Boone isn't sympathetic, but Shannon is drunk and free of inhibitions. She tells Boone that she knows he brought the money because he's in love with her and always has been. He tells her she's delusional, but can't resist when she kisses him.

Later Boone sits on the bed in the dark brooding. Shannon turns on the light and tells him that when they return to L.A. things will just go back to the way they were. She tells him to get dressed and that's the end of it.

Analyze This
A Statement About Sayid: Locke tells Boone not to make Sayid angry because, "We're going to need him on our side." What does this mean? Locke never says anything that

doesn't have meaning and seems to have a deep understanding of what is happening on the island. Is Locke alluding to a split or a war with the others? Either way he seems to believe that Sayid has the potential to turn against them.

Vision Quest: In many culture young boys engage in a vision quest right before they are considered adults. A vision quest always occurs in an altered state of mind whether from drugs or other means and is often lead by a medicine man or shaman. This journey for Boone may have been a vision quest because what Locke's "wacky paste" caused him to see was supposedly vital for his survival on the island. Was it a vision quest despite Boone's future? And is Locke a medicine man?

Signs & Symbols

Seeds: Although the trust between Jack and Kate has been shaken, the gift of seeds for Sun's garden symbolizes the possibility for new growth and fresh starts, perhaps for everyone else on the island as well.

Gift of Fish: As sustenance continues to be a theme in LOST, Hurley finds that there is no wall between himself and Jin when Jin rewards his efforts with a fish.

Walking off into the Darkness: At the end of the episode Boone and Locke walk away into the darkness of the jungle symbolizing the turn of Boone's path and the release of Shannon.

Listen to What the Fans Say:

The writers have acknowledged some influence by Stephen King's *The Stand*. This has lead many fans to look at the parallels. In The Stand many of the characters can be linked to LOST characters. For example in The Stand there is a reluctant hero (Jack?), a pregnant woman (Claire?), a woman with a questionable past and future (Kate?), a rock star (Charlie?) and a deaf mute (Jin?). These similarities have left fans wondering what will synch up in the storyline. The Stand is a story of Armageddon caused by a virus and the overall arch is both scientific and faith-based. Ultimately the story plays out as a religious battle of good against evil. Fans wonder if LOST will follow suit and who will end up on what side.

Truth & Speculation

- Jin says "I don't play with amateurs. Please go away," when Hurley asks to him to point him toward the fish

- Boone is tied up with a Japanese torture technique. The ropes have no knots, but are tied in such a way that when he reaches out with him arm, the one behind his back is yanked painfully.

- The writers say that the glimpse of the monster when it grabs Shannon is a clue to what it actually is.

Quotable Quips

- **Hurley** (to Boone about if he's hunting) I hope so, 'cause people need food, man. Solid food. This isn't a game, man.

- **Hurley** (to Jack about the leaves in his hand): Dude, these aren't for eating. Excuse me.

- **Jack** (to Kate): Please tell me you found a coffee bar.

- **Hurley** (to Jin): You're going to have to pee on my foot, man. It'll stop the venom. I saw it on TV. Ow, arrgh, no just pee on it man. Pee, pee on it. Pee on my foot. I'll lose my foot if you don't.

- **Charlie** (to Jack): Locke? The guy is a freak of nature, highly disturbed. Chances are, he probably killed all his mates at the post off ice the day his mom forgot to put a cookie in his lunch tin. That was my first impression anyway...and then he saved my life.

- **Locke** (to Boone): I gave you and experience that I believed was vital to your survival on the island.

Sawyerisms

To Australian police officer: Croc Hunter

Seven Degrees of LOST

Sawyer is being arrested behind **Boone** when he's speaking to the Australian police about Shannon.

Episode Fourteen: Special

Summary

Michael wakes up and Walt is gone. He went for a walk with his dog, but apparently didn't stay close. No one knows where he is. Michael looks for him frantically. The boy is in the jungle practicing throwing knives with Locke and Boone. His aim is terrible, until Locke tells him to use his mind's eye. Walt does as he's told and hits his target with amazing precision.

This is the scene that Michael walks into and he's not happy. He tells Walt to take Vincent back to camp. He's furious that Locke gave him a knife. Michael points the knife in Locke's face and Boone tackles him. Michael punches Boone and Locke pulls the men apart. Locke tries to calm Michael down and tells him that his son is special and should be allowed to realize his potential. Michael doesn't care. He threatens to kill Locke if he comes near his son again.

Everyone is noticing that Michael is having a hard time with Walt. Michael is also starting to realize that he does not want his son growing up on the island. He thinks they should build a raft and try to get off the islands. He finds Walt reading the Spanish comic book and tells him to come help him. Walt doesn't want to help.

Charlie is frantic to find Claire things from the beach and when he does moves them to a save place with him at the caves. When he begins to look through her stuff he finds that her diary is missing. There's only one person that could have taken it, Kate takes Charlie to confront Sawyer. Of course Sawyer has it, he's greedy for any type of reading material. He jokes that he's read it and harasses Charlie about his relationship with Claire, but in the end hands it over and hasn't read it at all. Charlie makes a valiant effort not to read it himself, but in the end succumbs to his curiosity.

Walt walks off again, claiming to be getting a drink of water, but goes to see Locke again. Locke explains that it's best to respect his father's wishes and stay away. Right then

Michael appears, furious. Walt is angry at his father for treating Locke poorly and tells him he's jerk. He also confronts him for never coming to visit. Michael doesn't care if he hates him, but the boy is going to listen to his father. Michael throws the comic into the fire and Walt watches it burn. Michael tells his son to stay put.

Hurley finds Michael to tell him that Walt has taken Vincent and left. Michael automatically assumes where the boy has gone, but he's wrong. Locke doesn't know where Walt is, but helps look for him. They find him trapped in a thicket of trees, a polar bear clawing at the thicket. Walt calls out to his dad.

Michael and Locke climb high above Walt and the polar bear, walking across tree branches and making their way to the thicket. Michael gets a knife from Locke and drops it down to Walt. He climbs down to Walt with some tree roots, wraps the around his son and Locke pulls him up. As Walt reaches safety, the polar bear attacks Michael. Michael stabs him in the chest and the bear runs away.

Sitting at the campfire that night, Michael gives Walt the box with all the letters he sent to him in the last eight years. Walt realizes that his mother never gave them to him, but Michael points out that she must have wanted him to have them because she never threw them away. Meanwhile Charlie has given in to temptation and is reading Claire's diary. He finds that she's been dreaming about "the Black Rock," the place the French woman spoke of, and wonders if Claire was taken there.

Out in the jungle, Locke is with Boone, using his whistle to try and call back Vincent. There is a rustle in the bushes and both realize that it's not the dog. Bracing for the worst, they are surprised to find Claire emerging. She is dirty, exhausted and shaken, but alive.

Michael Dawson 101

Michael and Susan look at cribs and the one Michael wants for his son costs three month's rent, but his son deserves the best. He mentions a friend of his could get him some construction work. Susan worries that he's giving up his art, but Michael assures her that it's only until she gets out of law school and gets a job, then she can support him and Walt. Susan is surprised at his choice of names for their son, but Michael would like to name his after his dad. Susan agrees, but only if he gets her last name. She apparently has no intention of marrying him.

Walt is a baby when Susan decides to leave. She's going to Amsterdam to work in international law. She says that she still loves him but it's too much of an opportunity to pass up. Michael tries to joke, offers to go to counseling, but she won't budge. Michael hasn't worked in months and Susan feels she can be the better provider. In fact they aren't married and no court would side with Michael.

Michael calls Susan in Amsterdam to talk to Walt, who's now twenty-one months old. He misses him. Susan seems distracted and there's a man talking in the background. Michael demands to know what's going on and Susan confesses that she is seeing someone, Brian Porter, the man that hired her. Michael is furious and yells into the phone that he's coming for his son. He slams down the phone and in his fury races across the street without looking. He is hit by a car.

In the hospital Michael works on a birthday card for his son. Walt is going to be two in a week. He's not sure what to put inside and his nurse suggests a joke. As the nurse leaves, Susan appears. She didn't know that he had been injured and had found out by calling a friend. Michael was hurt pretty badly and has a year of physical therapy to look forward to, but Susan tells him that she's covering all the costs. Michael's no dummy, he knows there must be a catch and it isn't hard to get it out of Susan. She's getting married to Brian, moving to Italy and Brian wants to adopt Walt. She asks Michael to stop thinking of himself and think of what's best for his son.

In Australia, Walt is much older and working on his homework on the living room floor. He's doing a report on Australian birds and has chosen the bronze cuckoo as his subject. He's trying to tell his mom and Brian about it, but their absorbed in their own conversation. Susan isn't feeling well. Walt calls out for them to look at him and what he's doing and they still ignore him. Walt is getting frustrated and suddenly a bird hits the window and kills itself, it's the same bird as pictured in Walt's book. Brian looks at Walt suspiciously.

Not long after Brian appears on Michael's doorstep. Susan died of a blood disorder and was only sick for about a week. He says that Susan asked that Michael have custody of Walt. Michael doesn't look convinces and for good reason. Brian admits he never really wanted to be the boy's father. Michael hasn't seen his son in nine years, but Brian wants him to just resume the relationship. Truth is there's something different about the boy that makes Brian uncomfortable. He says that "when he's around things happen." He leaves Michael with a roundtrip ticket to Australia and a one-way ticket from Sydney to New York.

In Australia, Michael waits for Walt to come home from school. The nanny gives him some of Susan's things that Brian asked to pass along to Michael, she also gives him a box that she thinks Walt should have. It's a small wooden box filled with all the cards he has sent him over the years.

Michael meets Walt and seems unsurprised when Walt refuses to go with him. When Walt asks for Brian, Michael swallows his pride and lies. He tells his son that Brian loves him, but has no choice but to let him go. Michael is Walt's legal guardian. He promises that Brian will call, write and visit. Walt can even take his dog. When Walt protests that the dog is Brian's, Michael assures him that Brian said he could have him.

Analyze This

The **comic book** that Walt is reading is a Flash and Green Lantern Comic and the pages read:

[The original PAGE 36 (the English version) reads:]

LEFT PANEL: Kyle Rayner is on an icy planet. He looks over his shoulder and
finds a polar bear on its hind legs right behind him.
THOUGHT BOX: Oh.
THOUGHT BOX: One of those bearskin rugs ...

THOUGHT BOX: ... with the bear still in it.

RIGHT PANEL 1: Kyle Rayner skids to a halt.
KYLE RAYNER (GREEN LANTERN): Oops

RIGHT PANEL 2: Kyle Rayner comes face to face with a polar bear.
POLAR BEAR SOUND: RRRRRRRR
KYLE RAYNER (GREEN LANTERN): Heh. My, what Big Teeth you have.
THOUGHT BOX: Won't Wally look smug when he finds out I wound up as Polar Bear
Food.
THOUGHT BOX: I won't give him the satisfaction.

RIGHT PANEL 3: Kyle lifts up his ring and points it at the polar bear.
THOUGHT BOX: Or let down Jay and Alan.
KYLE RAYNER (GREEN LANTERN): I think you need to be reminded ...

END OF PAGE
RESUME TO SCENE

(Walt turns the page.)

(The next page is of Jay Garrick, The Flash, and Alan Scott, Green Lantern,
talking with alien. The words are entirely in Spanish.)

[The original PAGE (the English version) reads:]

TOP LEFT CORNER FRAME: Close-up of hands on keyboard control panel.
SOUNDS: "Chek", "Vneep"
THOUGHT BOX: ... to do something about it.

MAIN CENTER PANEL: [CHAPTER THREE] Alien X talks with Jay and Alan.
JAY GARRICK (FLASH): What are you planning to do? What's the harm in telling
us that much? We're only Puppets to you anyway.
ALIEN X: Dying - is what I am doing. Because of Gunther,

because of you, I am
riddled with disease. But I will share my pain.
ALAN SCOTT (GREEN LANTERN): We understand how you
must feel. What we did half
a century ago, it was wrong, and what's been done to you since is
beyond
forgiveness. But if someone has to pay for that ...

LOWER RIGHT PANEL 1: Close-up of Jay and Alan.
JAY GARRICK: Let it be us.
ALAN SCOTT: No innocents need to be hurt.

LOWER RIGHT PANEL 2: Close-up of Alien X who holds
something in his hands.
ALIEN X: Innocents? What would this world know of Innocence,
when it --

LOWER RIGHT PANEL 3: Closer of Alien X who turns around.
ALIEN X: --What?
SOUNDS: Kra-Chung

The story line is about an encounter with aliens who the

heroes believe to be evil but ultimately turn out to be

misunderstood and good. Is this possibly a foreshadowing to

the truth of the others?

Signs & Symbols

Letters: Letters in LOST symbolize things unsaid or

undone. Sawyer's letter, as well as Michael's speaks to

unresolved past. Walt's reading of the letters may

foreshadow some resolution in their future.

Mind's Eye: The scene where Locke tells Walt to use his minds eye to aim with the knife mirrors the scene in Star Wars where Luke learns to use the force. Obi Wan instructs Luke to visualize his target and just like Walt makes his mark.

Saving Walt: When Michael saves Walt he at last acts as a father and the hero that we all want our father's to be. Michael puts himself in danger, making himself a sacrifice by putting himself in his son's place. Then he "slays the beast" and forgives Walt for running off. At last Walt has a father he can look up to.

Listen to What the Fans Say

Some fans wonder how much the story line of LOST hinges on Walt and his possible powers. The writers are big fans of Stephen King and Walt is very much like the little boy in *The Shining* and the girl in *Fire Starter*. He's a child and therefore has little control over his powers, but they are triggered by his emotions. The bird being killed and the polar bear appearing might both be manifestations of this power. Some fans even wonder if he somehow causes both his mother's death and the plane crash. Either way his powers may ultimately be critical to the story and Locke's mentorship seems imperative. Locke proves in the scene with the knife that with proper instruction, Walt to focus his power and manage it. Perhaps Walt's powers are responsible for getting them on the island and will ultimately be responsible for getting them off.

Truth & Speculation

- Harold Perrineau has starred in both Matrix sequels and the highly acclaimed HBO series Oz.

- Perrineau has a ten-year old daughter and Michael David Kelly often hangs out with Perrineau's family

- There are overall themes to the show but individual writers bring their own thematic material to each episode

Quotable Quips

- **Locke** (to Michael about Walt): As long as we're here I think he should be allowed to realize his potential.

- **Sawyer** (to Charlie, pretending to read Claire's diary): Dear Diary, I'm getting really freaked out by that has-been pop star. I think he's stalking me.

- **Boone** (to Shannon): Shannon, you've been a functioning bulimic since junior high. I thought you would be excited about dropping a size or two.

- **Charlie** (to Sayid about reading Claire's diary): Yeah I know, I'm bloody scum. Just listen to this.

- **Locke** (to Boone about the dog whistle):You can't hear everything, Boone. The sooner you learn that the better.

Sawyerisms

About Charlie: Has-been pop star

About Charlie: Little Limey Runt

Seven Degrees of LOST

Walt is **Michael's** son.
Locke recognizes **Walt**'s potential.

Episode Fifteen: Homecoming

Summary

Locke carries Claire back from the jungle, she's unconscious and Locke yells for Jack. Claire is fine, but she can't remember anything after getting on the plane to Los Angeles. Charlie gives her back her journal to help her remember.

Out in the jungle Charlie has a "conversation" with Jin. Suddenly they are attacked, Jin knocked out by rock from Ethan's slingshot. Ethan approaches Charlie and tells him that he want Claire back. Charlie tries to attack him, but Ethan is stronger. He threatens that unless Claire is brought to him, he will begin to kill the survivors one by one, killing Charlie last.

Locke has a plan. They can't track Ethan, he's too strong and dangerous. Locke sets four traps around the perimeter of the camp. Sayid prepares fires and men are set up to have sentry duty in rotating shifts. They will wait for him.

However, Boone falls asleep on his watch and a man on the beach is murdered. However it doesn't seem that Ethan got past anyone. It seems he came up from the sea.

There's concern amongst the rest of the survivors that Claire might be a plant from Ethan. Everyone is avoiding her or staring at her. Claire still doesn't remember anything and when Shannon tells her why everyone is treating her strangely, Claire is furious. She feels betrayed by Charlie and doesn't care if he was trying to protect her.

Locke and Jack are stumped on what to do. There seems to be no way for them to get the upper hand with Ethan. Jack has already told Kate that he won't open the Marshal's case and put guns in anyone's hands, but he changes his mind. There's no other choice. He takes a gun and gives Locke and Sayid one as well. Charlie wants to carry, but has no experience so they won't give him one. The only other suitable choice seems to be Sawyer. Kate wants to come as well, but they're out of weapons, until Sawyer hands over the gun he took from the Marshal's holster. Everyone's ready and despite Charlie's protests, they use Claire as bait.

Ethan arrives on cue and Jack bests him this time, even though he drops his gun. Everyone surrounds them, Ethan subdued and under control when shots ring out, and the captive falls to the ground, dead. Charlie has found Jack's gun and exacted his revenge.

Back at the camp, Claire comes to Charlie to tell him that she remembers peanut butter. Charlie smiles and tells her that it was imaginary peanut butter, actually. Claire still can't remember what happened to her, but she knows that she wants to trust Charlie.

Charlie 101

Charlie does the last of his drugs with his friend Tommy. They need to find a way to get another fix and Tommy has an idea. He takes Charlie to a bar where a young lady whose family frequents. Charlie starts a Drive Shaft song on the jukebox and makes his move. He charms Lucy Heatherton into a date. Afterward he also charms her into taking him back to her place and agrees to come back the next day for dinner with her father.

Lucy's father Frank is excited to have a rock star at his table, having set aside his own aspirations of musical success. Charlie admits that Drive Shaft is having more than a hiatus, the band might be dead. When Frank offers Charlie a job selling copiers for his company, Charlie accepts.

Tommy isn't very happy with this news. Charlie was only supposed to rob the Heathertons of something valuable enough to get him his next fix and pay off what he's been doing on speculation. Now Charlie has gotten involved instead. The problem with this, Tommy points out, is that his job starts in three days and by then he's sure to be reeling from the withdrawals.

Charlie is determined to give this job a shot. He memorizes the manual for the copier and dons the suit and briefcase that Lucy has gotten him as a gift. He's not looking so good though, and halfway through his first presentation he stumbles on the words. Then he vomits right into the copier.

Charlie tries to explain to Lucy that he's been down on his luck and wants to get better. However the gig is up. The EMTs that took Charlie to the hospital found a valuable cigarette case he had stolen form the house in his coat pocket. She understands that he's a junkie and why he would steal, but not why he agreed to take the job. Charlie confesses that he wanted to believe he could take care of her. Lucy assures him that he'll never take care of anyone and shuts the door.

Analyze This

Charlie's responsibility: Charlie seems to be motivated by his need to be responsible for those he cares about. Does this perhaps come from "failing" his younger brother? Charlie was unable to stop him from succumbing to the sex and drugs life of a rock star. Then ultimately his brother saved himself while Charlie fell further into the trap of this lifestyle. He wants to care for Lucy as well by fails. It is this deep desire to be responsible for Claire's well-being that brings him to kill Ethan. Charlie can't risk the possibility of Ethan finding a way to harm her again. In a way he sacrifices his soul to this purpose. Has Charlie taken a wrong turn with the right intentions and will this lead to his further fall in other episodes?

Signs & Symbols

Pariah: A pariah is a social outcast and a character that is commonly used in literature. Being ostracized from the group normally has grave consequences and is something that no one can afford to be in LOST. Claire sacrifices herself for the good of her tribe in order to avoid the status of pariah.

Truth: The truth continues to be an important theme in LOST. Charlie nearly smashes Claire's fragile trust by omitting the truth about Ethan's threats. He may have been able to have a relationship with Lucy if he hadn't omitted the truth about being a junkie. Omissions of truth foreshadow huge consequences.

Common enemy: Having a common enemy is often what brings tribes and countries together despite individual differences. This is the first instance of Kate, Sayid, Jack, Sawyer and Locke all working together without division.

Listen to What the Fans Say

The "Sceve" conspiracy has many fans wondering. Although Hurley gives a eulogy to Scott, fans with sharp eyes noticed that the actor that plays Scott is standing in the background at the "service." Does this mean that it was actually Steve that was buried and Scott is now assuming Steve's identity? It seems that the writers want not only the survivors of flight 815, but the audience as well to be confused. It is possible that Scott/Steve play a bigger role in the mystery than the average viewer might think. As the characters' stories are further developed, there is much synchronicity and interlinking in their storylines. This is probably true of all characters beyond the original fourteen that stand out. Perhaps Sceve will ultimately reveal a big piece of the island's mystery.

Truth & Speculation

- Dominic Monaghan has a tattoo that says, "Life is easy with eyes shut" a line from the Beatles, "Strawberry Fields Forever"

- The writers say they do in fact know where the show is going and have a "bible" despite rumors that LOST is being made up as they go.

- Charlie's character was originally a forty-five year-old washed up rock star, but they changed the part for Dominic Monaghan.

Quotable Quips

- **Charlie (**to Lucy Heatherton and friends)**:** Saucy sirens. I believe in monogamy. I will not be shared like a common curry.

- **Charlie** (to Jin): How nice it must be to not be involved in the bloody insanity that surrounds us at every turn. It's quite beautiful really. You take care of your wife, everything else is someone else's problem. No need to be involved in the decision −making process. No tree-shaking behemoths, French transmissions, just sweet bloody ignorance.

- **Kate** (to Jack): We're beyond sharpening knives here, Jack.

- **Hurley** (in eulogy to Scott): Scott Jackson worked for an internet company in Santa Cruz. He won a sales prize, a two week Australian vacation all expenses paid. He was a good guy. Sorry I kept calling you Steve, man. Um...amen, I guess.

- **Locke** (to Jack about Ethan): to him we're nothing more than a bunch of scared idiots with sharp sticks.

Sawyerisms

To Jack: Hoss

To Ethan: Jungle Boy

Seven Degrees of LOST

- **Scott** and **Steve** are friends that are often confused for one another and Scott has been killed. (or was it Steve?)

- **Ethan** is an Other and is killed.

- **Charlie** was the love interest of **Lucy Heatherton.**

Episode Sixteen: Outlaws

Summary

Sawyer wakes from a nightmare of his parents' death, opening his eyes and hearing sound like a boar. He looks around and there is a boar, a boar in his tent, rifling through his stuff. When he shines a light on it, the boars just stares him down. Sawyer picks up a stick and swing at it. The boar takes off running and takes the tarp from his tent with it.

It runs through the beach camp, Sawyer close on its tail, but Sawyer loses it in the jungle. On the way back he hears whispering, a man distinctly saying, "It'll come back around."

In the morning goes off looking for it and although he finds his tarp, there's no sign of the boar. He hears the man's whisper again and turns to see the boar. The boar runs at him and knocks him over. There's no doubt in Sawyer's mind now that the boar has a vendetta with him.

Back in the jungle he tries to track it attempting to hunt it. Kate catches up with him and points out his ineptitude at tracking. She offers to help if he will give her carte blanche, a blank check for anything in his stash. Sawyer doesn't like the deal, but wants the boar and takes it.

That night at a campfire, they play "I never" with some alcohol Sawyer procured from the plane. The game reveals that they have much in common and perhaps most importantly that both have killed a man.

While they have been sleeping, the boar has caught up to them. It left Kate's things alone, but ate all of Sawyers stuff and peed on his shirt. Locke appears, having noticed their trail and makes them coffee. He tells Sawyer a story about his sister dying, his mother blaming herself and a golden retriever that arrived at their door just after. He says that the point isn't that it was his sister, but that his mother thought it was. Because of this she was able to make peace with herself.

Jack has reclaimed all the guns from the battle with Ethan, with the exception of Sawyer's. Charlie may have given his back but he is quiet and withdrawn. He doesn't even crack a smile when Hurley jokes with him as they bury the body. Hurley is worried and asks Sayid to pay him a visit. Sayid talks to him and reminds him that sometimes even doing the right thing haunts you and that he should remember that he's not alone.

Kate and Sawyer go back to tracking and find a wallow. There's a squealing sound in the bushes and Sawyer reaches in to grab a piglet. Shaking the piglet he calls for the daddy pig and this angers Kate. She doesn't want it to get hurt. When Sawyer doesn't listen she kicks him in the shin, dropping Sawyer who in turn drops the piglet. Kate leaves him to find his own way home.

Sawyer is trying to find his way back, but is obviously lost. He yells for Kate and suddenly the boar is standing in front of him. He pulls his gun and cocks it, pointing it at the boar. The animal doesn't flinch, instead they stare each other down. Finally Sawyer lowers the gun and lets it go. He turns to see Kate is watching, stating that it's just a boar and they head back to camp. Back at the camp, Sawyer gives Jack back the gun. As they talk Jack says something that makes Sawyer realize that the man in the Australian bar drinking with him was Jack's dad, but Sawyer keeps it to himself.

Sawyer 101

A young Sawyer is awakened by his mother. There is someone pounding on the door and she looks distressed. His mother tells him to hide under the bed that the man pounding on the door will think he's at his grandparents. He makes him promise not to make a sound or to come out and tells him she loves him.

Sawyer can't see much from his hiding place but he can hear his mother and father arguing. It sounds like it's getting violent and then there's a gunshot and the sound of his mother's body falling to the floor. His father comes into the room, sits on the bed and again the sound of a gunshot rings out, the bed creaking with the weight of the fallen body.

Sawyer is an adult and making out with a woman in a hotel room. The light clicks on and another man, Hibbs, is sitting in the corner. Sawyer asks his lady to leave for a bit and starts a conversation that isn't friendly. Hibbs is there to make things even from the Tampa job. He has found the man that is responsible for his parents' demise. His name is Frank Duckett and he runs a shrimp truck in Sydney.

Sawyer gets a gun in Australia and goes to meet Duckett. Sawyer orders some shrimp from his truck and engages in some friendly conversation. He seems like a nice guy and Sawyer can't take it, he leaves.

Drinking in a bar he meets up with Jack's father, also drowning his misery. Christian tells Sawyer the shame he feels for himself and the pride he feels for his son. Christian suggests that whatever business Sawyer has he should finish it. Christian can't and knows he's paying for it.

Back at the shrimp truck, Sawyer finds Duckett again. This time he doesn't give him an opportunity to start a conversation, he shots him. Sawyer starts to read the letter to him, but Duckett swears he never went by the name Sawyer. As he dies he asks his killer to tell Hibbs he would paid. Sawyer is surprised at the mention of Hibbs and Duckett gets it. Sawyer has been duped. His last words are, "It'll come back around."

Analyze This

Redemption or Repetition: Does the island give everyone the opportunity to relive the parts of their lives they regret and make a different decision? Charlie gets the opportunity to give up drugs and to do right by Claire. Jack gets the opportunity to put what's better for an individual above his moral beliefs when he kills the Marshal. And in this episode Sawyer gets the opportunity to face Duckett again and decide whether or not to kill him. Will these new decisions, whether better choices or worse, make a difference on their future on the island?

Fate versus Design: Christian Shephard's ideology of "that's why the Sox will never win the series" demonstrates his idea that fate has doled out who he is and he can't change it. Jack thoroughly disagrees with this sentiment, believing in a tabula rasa in which men can become what they choose. Fate versus design is a common argument on the island. Why is correct?

Signs & Symbols

Boar: The boar is an obvious representation of Sawyer's guilt and an opportunity to face it.

Burying Ethan: Burying a man you killed is a symbol of respect for the death if not for the man. Charlie is facing the fact that this death was his responsibility and he is going to have to carry it with him.

It'll Come Back Around: Rather than a curse on Sawyer, this statement is a belief in karma and foreshadowing of what's to come. Hibbs will get his and so will Sawyer.

Listen to What the Fans Say

Some fans speculate that the island might somehow be linked to the story of the Philadelphia Experiment. Supposedly in 1943 the US government conducted a test with the USS Eldridge to see if electricity and the link between gravity and magnetism could be used to make the ship invisible. The ship was gone from the harbor for four hours and when it returned all the sailors were either dead or sick or worse. Could someone have been conducting some sort of "Philadelphia Experiment" on the entire island? Perhaps the plane was somehow affected and that's why it disappeared off the radar? Maybe the entire island appeared from another time and space because of the experiment. According to accounts of the USS Eldridge, the ship was never the same and perhaps this island and its oddities will never be the same either.

Truth & Speculation

- Josh Holloway is starring in an upcoming movie called, "Whisper"

- They often had to use CGI boars on the show because the real ones wouldn't work.

- The woman in the hotel room is Harold Perrineau's wife. When asked how he felt about his wife shooting a love scene with Josh Holloway, Harold joked "It *was* a little weird, so what I did was, I talked to the writers, and I said if *she's* gonna kiss him, then *I'm* gonna kiss him, so it was great! Josh is a really good kisser!"

Quotable Quips

- **Sayid** (to Sawyer about the boar running off): With your tarp? Perhaps he wanted to go camping.

- **Kate** (to Sawyer): Would you listen to yourself? It's a boar. Just go tell Locke, he'll kill it.

- **Hurley** (to Charlie about Ethan rising from the dead): Dude, I know how this works. This is gonna end with you and me running through the jungle, screaming and crying. He catches me first because I'm heavy and I get cramps.

- **Kate** (to Sawyer): Bottoms up, sailor.
- **Sawyer** (about the boar): Son of a ...oh! He peed on my shirt. He took my shirt out of the bag and peed on it. And you say this ain't personal.

Sawyerisms

- **To Sayid:** Genius
- **To Sayid:** Mohammed
- **To Kate:** Boar Expert
- **To Kate:** Sassafras
- **To the Bartender:** Slim
- **To Jack:** Sheriff

Seven Degrees of LOST

- **Sawyer** met **Christian Shephard** in a bar in Australia

- **Sawyer** killed **Frank Duckett**, thinking he was the original Sawyer

- **Sawyer** is connected to **Hibbs** through a con gone bad.

- **Mary Jo** is Sawyer's one night stand.

Episode Seventeen: ...In Translation

Summary

Jin finds Sun on the beach in a bikini and is furious. He yells at her and tries to cover her up while she responds with incredulity. As Jin tries to lead her back to camp, Sun trip and falls. Michael is watching and doesn't like what he's seeing. He tells Jin to get his hands off her. Jin yells back in Korean and they are about to get into a shoving match, when Sun slaps Michael across the face. Sun storms away with Jin following but suspicious, leaving Michael perplexed.

Sun finds Michael later and apologizes to him in English. She explains that she was protecting him, that he doesn't know what he husband is capable of doing. Michael knows he should have stayed out of their personal business and tells Sun that her husband is her problem not his.

Shannon helps Sayid work on Michael's boat. She's tying wood pieces together with perfect bolin knots. Sayid is impressed and they joke about it. Then Shannon invites him to spend a night alone with her.

The boat is coming together quickly, although Walt seems to have little interest in helping his father work on it. Jack asks who's going, knowing that the boat can only hold four. He's surprised to find that one of the other two people will be Sawyer who has "bought" his way on to the boat with a cable that will be used as a halyard.

Unfortunately, someone sets the boat on fire. Everyone runs to help put it out, but Michael is immediately pointing fingers. He is certain that Jin is the culprit. It doesn't help his case when Sawyer captures him, bringing him to Michael and they discover his hands are burned.

Sayid tells Boone that he's pursuing a relationship with Shannon out of respect. Boone, however can't help but disrespect his sister. He warns Sayid that she likes older men that will take care of her and that she'll discard him just like all the rest. This cools Sayid's ardor and Shannon notices. Looking for Boone, she finds Locke and asks him to tell her brother to stay out of her business. Locke suggests that she not give him the attention that she wants, she is free to pursue whomever she likes. The island offers a new life and Shannon should take it.

The evidence against Jin seems damning and he cannot speak his defense in English. Michael engages in a fist fight with him and no one will let Jack get in the middle of it. Jin isn't doing well and Michael isn't letting up. Then Sun appears and screams in English for them to stop. Everyone is floored that she can speak English and stop to listen.

Sun says that Jin didn't do it, that the raft was already on fire when he got there. No one is really buying the story until Locke steps up and points to the obvious. They are not alone on the island. The real enemy is the Others. The survivors listen and let Jin go.

Back at the caves Jin packs his bags, refusing to speak to Sun. She pleads with him to stay. She begs him to speak, but he ignores her. When she asks if they could start all over he finally says, "It's too late."

The raft is unsalvageable, but Michael is determined to rebuild. Walt asks if he can help and Michael of course agrees. But Locke sees through Walt. In private he asks why Walt set the raft on fire and Walt admits that he doesn't want to leave. Locke understands, he doesn't want to leave either.

Jin joins Michael at the boat with an axe, some bamboo and one word of English, "boat." Michael seems to agree to his help. Shannon has asked Sayid to allow her to start over. Charlie and Claire are sharing a meal. Sun stands in the ocean water in her bikini, face to the sky. Hurley watches all of this while he listens to his CD player and suddenly the battery dies and the music cuts out.

Jin-Soon Kwon 101

Jin waits in front of Mr. Paik, Sun's fathers, while he works at his desk. The man asks without looking up why he wants to marry his daughter. Jin explains that he has ambitions. He wants to own a restaurant and a hotel. When the man asks what Jin's father thinks, Jin tells him that he is dead. Mr. Paik asks if he would work for him and Jin says yes in such a way that Mr. Paik agrees to the marriage.

Before their wedding, Jin and Sun are giddy, although Sun is disappointed to hear that there will be no honeymoon. Jin will be going to work right away. Sun tells Jin that it is a shame his father isn't alive to see this day.

It isn't long before Mr. Paik calls Jin into his office. Jin thinks he's about to be reprimanded, but instead Mr. Paik promotes him, to special assistant. He tells him his first assignment will be to go to the home of Byung Han, the Secretary for Environmental Safety and give him a message. Mr. Paik is displeased.

Jin does as he's told. He simply gives the man the message. Byung seems distressed at Jin's arrival and then relieved upon receipt of the message. He's so relieved in fact that he gives Jin his daughter's dog, a champion pedigree as a gift. Jin leaves confused.

Jin arrives home for dinner one night and Sun has prepared him a feast. He wants to spend a quiet evening with her and ignores his cell phone when it rings. When the land line rings as well he has no choice but to take it. It's Sun's father. His factory has been closed, which can only mean that Jin did an incompetent job of delivering the message. Mr. Paik tells him that he will be driving one of his associates to Byung Han's house and the man will demonstrate how to deliver a message correctly.

Jin drives the man there, but it immediately becomes apparent that it's an assassination mission. Jin goes in the house before the other man. He beats Byung Han mercilessly in front of his wife and children, but manages to save him from being shot.

When Jin arrives back home, bloody and disheveled, Sun is immediately concerned. She follows him into the bathroom, but he won't tell her what he's done. He only says that he does what her father tells him to do and continues to coldly wash his hands. When Sun leaves the bathroom, Jin begins to cry.

At a pier, Jin watches an old man with a small boat. When he approaches, the man greets him warmly and Jin immediately begins to apologize. It is his father and he asks for forgiveness for being ashamed of him. They talk and Jin tells him of his beautiful intelligent wife and that their marriage has gone sour. Sun's father is an evil man and he cannot tell her this. Jin want to start over and his father suggests that he can. Once Jin delivers the watches to his associates in Sydney and Los Angeles, Jin should run away with Sun to America and never come back.

Analyze This

Hurley's batteries: His batteries couldn't last forever or viewers would have complained. However, the writers could have picked any episode to have them die. Why this one? Did the death of Hurley's music foreshadow darker times to come? Perhaps the time to hide beneath headphones and wish for life before the island is over. Perhaps this was a final indicator that no one is coming for them.

194

Burning the raft: Locke seems to be the observant voice of reason on the island and the only one who guesses that Walt burned the raft. Yet he only asks the boy why and then seems to agree with his reasoning. Will Locke find ways to try to keep them on the island as well? He seems to have good reason for staying.

Signs & Symbols

Fire: Fire is symbolic of destruction, the symbolism of chaos and war. Fire burns everything, bringing nothing but ruin. And yet, Prometheus risked the wrath of the Titans to bring fire to man. Fire also banishes the darkness and can be used as a signal for help. Fire cleanses and purifies. Lastly, sometimes Love is spoken of as an eternal flame. Like so many things on the island, fire is a dichotomy.

Language: Language is the key to working together. Castaways thrown together in literature always forge some sort of language, like Robinson Crusoe and Friday in Daniel

Defoe's book. Jin's separation from Sun will force him to engage and at last forge a language.

Father Figures: Literal and figurative father figures play a huge role in LOST. In this episode, Locke reveals that he has issues with his father. Walt is learning to embrace his father. Jin had at least embraced his father before he left for Sydney. Father's are ideally a figure that guides us and all the characters in LOST are seeking guidance.

Listen to What the Fans Say

Another theory is that the island is a sort of Noah's ark. Scientists studying the Earth's magnetic field have noted that there might be a polar reversal in the near future. If this were to happen, the Earth would lose its magnetosphere and be vulnerable to massive radiation form the sun. What if the island is an environment designed for the survival of the human race if such an event were to occur. The island could be prepared with an artificial magnetosphere (a concept alluded to in the Flash/Green Lantern comic) and the appropriate people found or even genetically engineered to be the Adam and Eve's of the new human race. The appropriate founders would have diverse backgrounds and talents, just like those that are now currently on the island.

Truth & Speculation

- LOST is the first time Danielle Dae Kim has spoken his native language, Korean in an acting roll.

- The actors only know what's happening with their own characters stories and only as the story is shot.

- The LOST staff is aware that it is unlikely that everyone would remain so well groomed on the island, but knowing their viewers like attractive characters, assume the audience will suspend their belief.

Quotable Quips
- **Locke** (to Shannon): Everyone gets a new life on this land, Shannon. Maybe it's time to start yours.

- **Hurley** (when Sun speaks English): Didn't see that coming.

- **Locke** (about the burned raft): They've attacked us! Sabotaged us, abducted us, murdered us. Maybe it's time we stop blaming us and start worrying about them.

- **Michael** (to Walt): Come here. Look, we all have setbacks. I mean, God know, man, that's just life. We'll start over, right?

- **Sun** (to Jin): I was going to leave you! I was going to get away. But you made me change my mine. You made me think you still loved me.

Sawyerism
To Jin: Chief

To Jin: Bruce

To Sun: Betty

Seven Degrees of LOST
Hurley is on the TV having won the lottery at Byung's house.

Jin is a strong arm for **Sun**'s father.

Episode Eighteen: Numbers

Summary

Michael works on the new boat with Jin and Hurley. Michael asks Jack for help making something that can send out a distress call. Jack says he'll ask, but they're going to need something to power it. Talking to Sayid, Jack and Hurley suggest the French woman as a source for batteries. Sayid refuses to tell them where she is. She's not going to welcome them with open arms. While Jack and Sayid argue, Hurley finds a piece of paper that has numbers scribbled on it by Danielle, over and over the same numbers Hurley used to win the lottery.

It's bothering Hurley and he wakes Sayid in the middle of the night to ask him about the numbers. Sayid thought they might be coordinates, but now he's not sure. It's not enough of an answer for Hurley he has to find out. So he steals Sayid's map, packs up in the morning and leaves.

Sayid accuses Jack of sending Hurley to steal the map and when he realizes that Hurley has gone solo, they both go looking for him. Charlie says he ran into him earlier and he was acting strange and heading out for a walk. There's no doubt now, Hurley has gone to look for Rousseau and the other three men go after him.

Hurley finds the cable on the beach and starts following it into the jungle. Hurley starts to see remnants of the traps on his way in and then hears the squeak of metal under his feet. He stops and hears Sayid yelling at him not to move. He's standing on a pressure plate that will release a nasty looking branch covered with pikes. The three men start to work out a plan, but Hurley decides he can get off it and out of the way. Despite everyone's protests, he jumps. The trap misses him and gets up to move on calmly, he's there to get a battery.

Right when the cable ends, Charlie finds a rickety rope bridge stretched across a chasm. It doesn't look like it can hold anyone, let alone Hurley would steps right on it and starts crossing. Hurley makes it safely across and Charlie follows after him, encouraged. Halfway there the bridge begins to snap. Charlie just barely makes it as the bridge falls away. Jack tells them to stay put while he and Sayid find another way across. Hurley won't hear it. There's a path in front of him and he's following it.

Sayid and Jack find Rousseau's shelter, but it's booby-trapped and is blown to smithereens. There's nothing there anyway. It looks as though she relocated and set it up for whenever Sayid brought someone back.

Charlie and Hurley hear the blast and start to head back to where they heard it. Charlie is angry at Hurley for his odd behavior which is putting everyone in danger. He demands an explanation. Hurley starts to give him one, but is interrupted by gunshots. Rousseau has found them. Charlie gets away, but not Hurley. Rousseau has a rifle to his head, but Hurley has to know. What do the numbers mean? When Danielle doesn't have an answer, Hurley loses it. He's tired of being mister nice guy, he wants answers.

Danielle seems to understand his desperation and lowers her gun to tell him the story. Her crew picked up a transmission, the numbers coming from the island. They changed course to investigate and shipwrecked. They found the radio tower, but her crew became sick and died before they could unravel the mystery. Rousseau changed the transmission. This isn't enough. Hurley wants to know why they are cursed. They are cursed right?

Danielle gives it some thought. The numbers are responsible for her losing everything she loved, so yes, they must be cursed. Hurley is so relieved and thankful that he begins to cry. Finally, someone believes him. Someone understands. He scoops Danielle up into a crushing hug.

Charlie finds Sayid and Jack, but they aren't sure where Hurley is. Knowing that Charlie escaped Rousseau's gun fire they are thinking the worst. Then Hurley shows up, with a battery.

Locke goes to Claire and asks her to help him build something. The work on all day, but Claire has no idea what they're building. She thinks its maybe a trap for an animal. It's kept Claire occupied all day and there is much she doesn't want to think about, so she's grateful for the diversion. In fact, it's her birthday. What she doesn't realize is that she is helping Locke make her birthday present. When he flips it over, the end result is obvious, a baby cradle.

At a campfire that night, Charlie sits next to Hurley, wanting to finish the conversation that was interrupted by gun fire. Hurley tells him that his luck might have caused the plane crash. Charlie thinks this is ridiculous and trumps him with his story of drug abuse. Now Charlie want to know Hurley's big secret. When Hurley tells him he's worth $156 million, Charlie thinks he's joking and walk away grumbling. ---Meanwhile, a close up of the hatch reveals a particular series of numbers that are all too familiar to Hurley.

Hugo "Hurley" Reyes 101

Hurley flips through the channels looking for the lottery draw while his mother harasses him from the kitchen. Mary Jo, the lotto girl, calls out the numbers and stats that it's a near record jackpot. Hurley looks at the ticket in his hand and passes out.

Hurley has won a lot of money, but everything else seems to be going badly. During an interview with the press his grandfather has a heart attack and dies. The priest at the funeral gets struck by lightening. His brother's wife leaves him for another woman. His mother breaks her ankle outside of the new house Hurley bought her, which is burning down. And to add insult to injury, Hurley is mistaken for a drug dealer and arrested.

Despite this rash of bad luck, Hurley's accountant is doing amazing things with the winnings. His interest in California orange futures has sky rocketed due to storms in Florida. He's the majority shareholder for a box company in

Tustin. His sneaker factory in Canada burned down, but was over insured and will lead to windfall of cash. Not to mention the settlement for the LAPD. When his accountant asked where he got his numbers, Hurley is realizes that it's not the money, but the numbers that are jinxed. The accountant tries telling him he's crazy as a man falls, screaming past the office windows.

Hurley goes on a mission to figure out the problem with the numbers and starts where he heard them, in the mental institution. He meets with Lenny who initially ignores him, but perks up when he hears Hurley used the numbers Lenny goes ballistic telling him he's opened the box, that's he's got to get away from the numbers. As the orderlies drag away the agitated man, Hurley gets out of Lenny that he got the number from Sam Toomey in Kalgoorie, Australia.

Hurley goes to Sam Toomey's house in Australia and his wife answers the door. Unfortunately, Sam has been dead for four years, but his wife knows all about the numbers. Sam and Lenny were in the navy, stationed at a listening post monitoring long wave transmissions. One night they heard the numbers. Couple of days later Sam was at a fair with his wife and used the numbers to guess how many beans were in a huge jar. They won and got in a car accident on the way home. Martha, his wife, lost her leg. Sam walked away without a scratch. Bad things started happening all around him and he moved them out into the middle of nowhere. Sam was sure he was cursed and ultimately ended it by shooting himself with a shotgun. Martha chastises Hurley for believing there's a curse on the numbers. She still thinks the idea of it is ridiculous.

Analyze This

Games: There is much significance to games in LOST. We meet Locke first over a backgammon game, the theme of backgammon pieces as black and white, light and shadow continues to crop up. Backgammon demonstrates Walt's uncanny good luck. Could Connect Four be another important game? It seems to be connected to the lottery numbers, as Lenny drops pieces into the game while compulsively repeating the numbers. What is the correlation between the two games? What is the correlation between Walt's good luck and Hurley's bad luck?

Was Hurley Committed?: Hurley went to the Santa Rosa institute to visit Lenny and Dr. Curtis knew him. Hurley obviously got the numbers from listening to Lenny, so both things indicate that he spent time there. He's living with his mother, which seems to be something his mother wants based on their conversation. And when Hurley wins the lottery, he tells the press he's put his family through a lot recently and wants to do something for them. Was he committed? If so why? What happened to Hurley before he used the numbers?

Signs & Symbols

Pandora's Box: When Hurley tells Lenny that he has used the numbers for the lottery, Lenny cries out that he has opened the box. Although there may be an actual box in the show (perhaps he even means the hatch), metaphorically this statement also refers to the mythical box that Pandora couldn't resist opening, releasing all possible evils into the world.

The Labors of Hurley: In mythology heroes often have to perform labors or trials in order to achieve their ultimate goal. Mirroring a mythical hero, Hurley outsmarts another hero for the map, leaps out of harms way to avoid a trap, traverses a dangerous bridge, and in the end gets the necessary information out of the oracle.

Hurley as the Every Man: Hurley is the character that represents the audience, the one that comments on what the audience might be thinking, much like a Greek Chorus. Through Hurley viewers are able to insert themselves in the story and imagine that they are on the island as well.

Listen to What the Fans Say

Is it possible that the survivors of flight 815 were "unbreakable" like the premise of Bruce Willis' character in the move Unbreakable? That movie was based on comic mythos and the writers are familiar and comfortable with the genre. The weight that is placed on the comic book that Walt is reading would lend to this interpretation as well. The survivors don't have to be invulnerable, but perhaps they are somehow super humans and that explains why they were able to survive the crash as well as why they heal so fast. Perhaps Jack is being groomed to be the superhero and Locke the villain? Just like in Unbreakable there must be a black and white, a clearly good and evil.

Truth & Speculation

- Jack's seat was 23a.
- According to modern philosopher Robert Anton Wilson, the number 23 is a part of the cosmic code

and connected with so many synchronicities and weird coincidences that it must mean something.

- Jorge Garcia was asked to audition for LOST based on a stand out performance as a pot dealer in *Curb Your Enthusiasm*.

Quotable Quips

- **Hurley** (guessing what Jin is gesturing) You want to make snowballs?

- **Hurley** (about his luck) And at the funeral, Father Aguilar getting struck by lightening. Man, that was a freak storm. And Diego moving back home after Lisa left him for that waitress.

- **Charlie** (about Hugo on the pressure trigger): Replace his weight? How are we going to do that?

- Hurley (to Charlie): I can get out of the way. I'm spry.

- **Charlie** (to Hurley): One minute you're happy-go-lucky good-time Hurley and the next you're Colonel Bloody Kurtz.

- **Hurley** (to Danielle) Okay, that thing in the woods, maybe its' a monster, maybe it's a pissed-off giraffe. I don't' know.

Sawyerisms

To Walt: Short Round

Seven Degrees of LOST

The Lottery Girl pulling the numbers on TV is **Mary Jo, Sawyer's** love interest.
Sam Toomey and **Leonard Sims** hear the numbers in a transmission.
Sam Toomey played the names and won $50,000 in a bean game.
The numbers are on the hatch.
Hurley owns the box company where **Locke** is an employee.
Danielle is "cursed" by the same numbers as **Hurley.**

Episode Nineteen: Deus Ex Machina

Summary

Locke and Boone are still trying to figure out how to get into the hatch. Locke has built a trebuchet, which should deliver a half a ton of force to the hatch's window. He is certain that it will work. However, it barely leaves a mark. Locke is furious, so furious he doesn't notice the piece of shrapnel in his leg. It's a bamboo shard, deeply embedded and Locke pulls it out, seemingly not feeling a thing. When he tries to inflict pain on leg later with a pin and fire, he can't feel anything either. This is worrisome, but John is still focused on opening the hatch.

Locke has a dream that he is telling Boone the island will give them a sign and sees a small airplane crash. Boone is staring at the sky suddenly covered in blood. Locke's mother appears also pointing at the plane. Then Boone begins to chant, "Theresa falls up the stairs. Theresa falls down the stairs." Locke is suddenly back in his wheelchair and begins to yell, panicking. Then Locke wakes up and knows what to do.

It's early, but he wakes up Boone. They have to get going. Locke tells him about his dream and about Boone's chant. Boone is unnerved, but wonders if he mentioned Theresa some other time. Locke is suddenly having difficulty with his leg, but refuses to admit that anything is wrong. Before Boone can press him further on the issue, they discover a man who is long dead and dressed as a priest hanging from a tree.

Locke is certain this means the plane is somewhere nearby and they move on. Locke can't move easily though, the leg is getting worse. Boone wants to take him back to Jack, but Locke refuses. He finally admits that he was paralyzed before the crash. The island gave him back his legs and although it's taking them away again, he has to trust it. Boone helps him up and the keep moving. Boone has his own confession. Theresa was his nanny and his favorite pastime was calling her up the stairs to his room from the intercom. When he was six, Theresa fell coming up the stairs and broke her neck.

As Boone tells Locke his story Locke looks up and hanging from the edge of the cliff is a small plane. Boone climbs up to see what's inside. The plane is positioned precariously and could fall at any moment. When Boone discovers there's nothing more than statues of the Virgin Mary filled with heroin, Locke yells to him to come down. Boone spies a radio though and ignores the groans and creaks of the shifting plane. He tries the radio and calls mayday. The plane is going though and Locke is yelling for him to come down. Boone can't, a man answers his transmission and he's riveted. The voice says the "We're the survivors of flight 815." Boone doesn't have time to ponder this because the plane come crashing down from the cliff.

Jin and Michael continue to work on the boat and the noise is really bothering Sawyer. He's getting headaches everyday and Kate is concerned. It takes some convincing, but she finally gets Sawyer to Jack and Jack to agree to look at him. Jack can't resist making light of the situation, asking Sawyer questions about his sex life in front of Kate. Sawyer isn't in any danger though. He just needs glasses. Going through the glasses left behind, they are able to design him a workable pair and fix his headaches.

Locke gets up, his legs aren't working well, but hurries to the fallen plane. He finds Boone inside. He's conscious, but his injuries look bad. Locke struggles and lifts Boone up over his shoulders and forces his legs to move toward the camp. He gets him to Jack telling him he fell from a cliff, but when Jack turns to ask Locke for more information, he has disappeared.

Back at the hatch Locke screams into the dark, pounding on the hatch. He has done everything he thought he was told to do and doesn't understand why this has all happened to him. As he cries against the darkened window of the hatch, a miraculous thing happens. The window lights up from within.

John Locke 101

John Locke is working in a toy store, showing a little boy how to play Mousetrap. A woman appears and asks where to get a football, staring as she walks away. Later when he gets into his car to leave, he sees the woman again. She realizes she's been seen and runs. Running after her, Locke is hit by a car, but only stunned. He gets back up and runs her down. She admits that she's his mother.

In a diner, Locke sits across the table from her, but tells her she isn't his mother. The woman is certain though, knows that he hasn't lived with his parents and when she says his father is still alive, Locke's interest is piqued. At least, it is until she tells him that he was immaculately conceived.

Locke hires a private investigator and discovers that the woman is indeed his mother and has been in and out of mental institutions. The investigator has found his father as well, but doesn't think it's a good idea to pursue the lead. Locke doesn't care, he wants the information.

Locke goes to his home, a large and gated property with a guard stationed outside. Locke asks to see Anthony Cooper, explaining that he's his son. The guard seems unconvinced, but calls Cooper who instructs him to let the man in. Locke is welcomed by his father who offers to take him hunting.

Locke has been hunting birds with is father frequently and arrives at his house for another day out in the field. When Locke enters the house he finds his father hooked to a dialysis machine, it seems he arrived an hour early. Anthony needs a kidney transplant and hasn't yet found a donor. The men continue to bond and there's little doubt of the outcome.

In the hospital father and son are prepped for the surgery, all smiles and jokes. When Locke wakes however, his father has been checked out to be in private care at home and has left no message. His mother arrives and gives Locke the hard truth. He was set up to give his father a kidney. She needed the money and Cooper was certain the only way Locke would agree to a transplant would be if it was his own idea.

Locke is crushed and desperate for this all to be a misunderstanding. He rips out his IV and drags himself out of the hospital. He drives to his father's, but the guard won't let him in. Locke is no longer welcome at his father's home. Locke drives away devastated with anger and pain.

Analyze This

Paralysis: Regaining the use of his legs has made Locke into the man he is now on the island. What would happen if he lost him mobility? And why is he losing mobility now? Is this the island "testing" him or is it all in his mind. As Locke remembers the wrongs that have been done to him by his father, perhaps his past is physically haunting him. Or perhaps the island again is proving that mysteries abound.

Special: Just like Brian tells Walt's father that the boy is special, Locke's mother tells him that he is special. The writers of the LOST are very deliberate and there is no doubt that this is a parallel. Does being "special" explain the affinity between Locke and the boy? And what exactly does "special" mean?

Signs & Symbols

Opening the hatch: To Locke, opening this door to the heart of the island symbolizes opening to gate to his father's home and to perhaps his own heart.

Voice of the Island: Perhaps there is a voice to the island that Locke can hear, but listening to the island symbolizes tapping into the collective consciousness and seeing the signs that lead us to our destiny.

MouseTrap: When Locke shows the boy in his flashback how to play MouseTrap, he both parallels and foreshadows the games that he is adept and playing and traps his able to set up on the island.

Hunting: When Locke hunts with his father he fulfills a need he seems to have carried his whole life to bond with a father figure. Hemingway, the most prominent hunter in literature was referred to as "Papa" and the hunt is male-bonding at it's more powerful. This makes the betrayal all the worse.

Listen to What the Fans Say

Although there is much discussion about the mysticism surrounding Locke, many argue that he is simply an intelligent man and an opportunist. He seems to be there every time a character has a key moment, but this is more about his own needs than the needs of others. Locke knows how to play the game and there is nothing mystical about that. He stacks his cards so that he will be properly positioned within the group regardless of the circumstances.

This means that Locke may come across as good or evil depending on what he deems the situation requires. There's no higher morality involved. Fans that argue this do not believe there is anything mystical about Locke's sudden mobility on the island. There are many explanations for the miracle of ambulation. It is possible that Locke has a herniated disc that slipped back into position during the physical trauma of the crash. He might also have had psychosomatic paralysis based on past traumatic experience. He kept his muscles from atrophying by utilizing the PRO ElectDT® electromedical device, so it's highly possible his muscles would work fine once Locke decided he wasn't paralyzed.

Truth & Speculation

- Damon Lindelof states that you can see everything about Locke's character in his first speaking scene with the backgammon set.

- When looking into the eyes of the "monster" Terry O'Quinn was told to imagine he was gazing on the most beautiful thing he had ever seen.

- According to the writers everything will have a rational and sci-fi explanation.

Quotable Quips

- **Locke** (to Boone): Then the island will tell us what to do.

- **Locke** (Boone): Don't tell me what I can't do.

- **Boone** (to Locke): have you been using that wacky paste stuff that made me see my sister get eaten?

- **Jack** (to Kate about Sawyer): All I'm going to get for my trouble is a snappy one-liner. And if I'm real lucky, a brand new nickname.

- **Michael** (to Jack about Jin): Yeah, I'm pretty sure I know how to say uh... faster and idiot.

Sawyerisms

None this episode.

Seven Degrees of LOST

Hurley is in the same institution as **Emily Locke,** just at a different time.

Anthony Cooper is the father of **John Locke.**

Episode Twenty: Do No Harm

Summary

Jack works on Boone, but it's not going well. He's trying to staunch the flow of blood and working with help that isn't medically trained. Then Boone's lung collapses. Jack pours peroxide on his chest and stabs a metal rod through, allowing air to pass through again. Jack runs a tube through the hole and sends Kate to go get Sawyer's alcohol. Jack tells Boone that he's going to save him.

Boone is getting worse though and Jack realizes he need blood, but first they've got to sort his leg. Sun and Jack put a smooth piece of wood between his teeth and snap the leg back into place. Boone screams.

On her way back with the liquor bottles from Sawyer, Kate trips and breaks a few in her backpack. This is the least of her problems. She hears whimpering and stumbles on Claire who is definitely in labor and unable to move. Kate yells for help and Jin arrives. Kate manages to get across to him that they need Jack and sends him off to give him the bottle and come back with the doctor. Kate stays with Claire.

Jack needs two things, something that will work as a needle and the right blood. Sun brings him sea urchin spines, which seem a promising solution. They manage to get out of Boone that he's A negative, but Charlie can't find anyone with that blood type. In fact most of the survivors don't even know their blood type. This leaves Jack with no choice. He's an O negative, a universal donor. The blood is going to have to be his.

Jack's blood is draining into Boone with Jin arrives. Sun translates and tells Jack that Claire is in labor, her contractions every two minutes. Charlie thinks he's going to go deliver the baby, but Jack has other plans. It's going to have to be Kate. She's going to have to direct Claire when to push and clear the baby's nose and mouth when it's born.

Boone apologizes to Jack for screwing up. He says something about a plane and a hatch that John didn't want him to tell anyone about. He knows that his prognosis isn't good. In fact his leg seems to be crushed and all the blood from Jack is pooling there. It's obvious that Locke was lying, Boone didn't fall; something fell on him.

Charlie returns with Jin to Kate and Claire with water and towels and explains that Kate is going to have to deliver the baby. Kate is terrified, but there's nobody else to do it. Kate goes to Claire and starts coaching. Claire resists, she doesn't want to give birth on the island, she's afraid the baby will know she was going to give it up, she's afraid of what Ethan might have done to it, but Kate calms her down and gets her to push.

Jack decides there is no other recourse than to amputate Boone's leg. Jack has Michael help him with moving Boone to the cargo container, a larger metal container with a heavy sliding door. It's going to have to make due as a guillotine. Sun tries to stop him. Boone's going to die anyway and she doesn't think this will help him to remove his leg. Jack is unwavering, until Boone wakes up and asks him to stop. He knows there's no chance to save him and he's letting Jack off the hook for his promise to do so.

Jack holds Boone in his arms and helps him settle back on the pallet he's lying on as Boone dies. In the jungle, Claire gives birth to a healthy baby boy.

When Claire brings her baby to the beach, the other survivors join her and rejoice. When Jack sees Shannon and Sayid returning from a romantic dinner alone, she approaches them to give them the news about Boone.

Shannon goes to Boone's body and cries, grieving the loss of her brother. Jack meanwhile cries alone on the beach. He's pleased about Claire's baby and devastated that he couldn't save Boone. Kate tries to get him to talk about the fact that Boone died, but Jack only says the he didn't die, he was murdered and Locke is responsible.

Jack Shephard 101

Jack is trying on tuxes with his best friend Marc Silverman. Marc is nervous about giving a toast, but it's Jack that is getting married.

At the pre-wedding luncheon, Sarah, Jack's fiancée gives a toast following Marc's. She reveals that two years ago she was in a car accident and broke her back. It was supposed to be irreparable, but Jack wouldn't give up. He fixed her and he's her hero.

The night before the wedding, Jack is waiting for his father and still trying to write his vows. He doesn't know what to write. Sarah offers to let him off the hook, but he wants to do it. When he father shows up late that night, Jack still hasn't written a word. He's not sure if he should marry Sarah, if he can be the husband and father that he wants to be. His dad's answer is cryptic. He tells Jack that his problem isn't commitment, but letting go. The next day at the wedding, Jack still hasn't written his vows and wings it instead. He says he hasn't been able to because he's not good at letting go. He tells Sarah that he didn't save her, she saved him and he will always love her.

Analyze This

Birth/Death: The island takes a life and gives on in return. Yet another example of the heightened duality of the place. Will the baby thrive? Will the island always gives as it takes? Or will the island slowly take the survivors one by one?

Letting Go: Christian tells Jack that his problem isn't committing, but rather, letting go. Jack takes this to me that he needs to "let go" in order to write his vows, but is that what his father really meant? Is Jack still hanging on to Sarah because she has become his responsibility on the basis of a promise? Is this why Jack is able to abide by Boone's wishes and let him go, because Boone relieves him of his promise to keep him alive?

Signs & Symbols

Blood: Life is in the blood and many of the survivors don't even know their own blood type. Jack knows his and even though he could be sacrificing every one on the island if he kills himself giving it, he'll do it. Jack's giving of blood is a reflection of his determination to follow through on his promises no matter what the cost.

Amputation: Many characters LOST have missing limbs, the farmer that helps Kate, Sam Toomey's wife and Boone nearly lost his leg. Missing limbs are an outward symbol of missing pieces of the soul, but Boone remains whole when he dies.

"Don't tell me what I can't do.": As Jack and Locke become foils for one another in LOST, their similarities and differences become more and more obvious. This is a phrase that both have said repeatedly. They are so much the same, but this episode creates an even further divide between the man of science and the man of faith.

Listen to What the Fans Say

Another theory that revolves around everyone on flight 815 being dead is that LOST is following the mythology of the Egyptian afterlife. The Egyptians believe they are born into another world called Amenti, where they would utilize the knowledge gained in this world. The afterlife is actually a struggle. You are newborn into Amenti and must slowly regain the use of your limbs in order to regain mobility. The newly born are allowed to play checkers, a game that is used to solve disputes. Then there is a series of trials that the dead must perform in order to stand trial and enter paradise. The trials involve demons that include those manifesting as black boars and evil fish. There are also damned souls in Amenti that are dangerous. Proponents of this theory point out that the mythology could be used to at least inform the storyline, if not encompass it.

Truth & Speculation

- Boone was originally named "five" a reference to him being Boone Carlyle V

- The writers were originally going to reveal the "monster" in this episode, but changed their minds because of the show's success.'

- Damon Lindelof states that the monster is NOT a dinosaur.

Quotable Quips

- **Marc Silverman** (to Jack about his toast): After about eight beers, I'll be fine.

- **Sarah** (toast to Jack): Because you fixed me, I will dance at our wedding. To Jack. My hero, Jack.

- **Charlie** (to Jack): I asked the whole sodding camp. No one knows their blood type. I don't know my bloody blood type.

- **Hurley** (to Jack after the transfusion): Woah, dude. You all right, man? You're looking kinda goth.

- **Christian** (to Jack): Commitment is what makes you tick, Jack. The problem is you're just not good at letting go.

- **Jack** (to Sun): Don't tell me what I can't do!

Sawyerisms

About Jin: Kato
To Claire: Mamacita

Seven Degrees of LOST

Sarah Shephard is **Jack**'s wife.
Mark Silverman is **Jack**'s best friend.

Episode Twenty-One: The Greater Good

Summary

Shannon mourns the loss of Boone and tells Sayid that Sun told her he wouldn't let Jack take his leg, that he didn't want to waste the antibiotics and he was brave. This information doesn't seem to be helping her much. She's silent at his funeral and when no one speaks, Sayid says a eulogy.

Locke appears when Sayid is finished and claim the blame for Boone's death. He tells the story of the Beechcraft and Boone's bravery trying to get to the radio. He says he couldn't go up because his leg was hurt so Boone went and the plane fell.

Jack can't take it. He starts screaming a Locke wanting to know what he did to Boone and why he lied about him falling from a cliff. Jack attacks him and the others pull him off. The exertion is too much for him and Jack wobbles and collapses.

Jack tells Sayid that Boone said something about a hatch and Locke is hiding something. Jack is exhausted and need rest but won't relax, so Kate puts some crushed sleeping pills in his juice and knocks him out.

Shannon goes to Sayid and asks him to do something about the fact that Locke killed her brother. Sayid finds Locke and has him take him to the plane. Sayid tries to get more information out of him as they walk through the jungle, but isn't very successful. He does however, find out that Locke was the one that knocked him out and destroyed his equipment when he was triangulating the signal. Still, Locke is coy about the hatch.

Sayid obviously doesn't trust Locke, but he also doesn't think he killed Boone. He tells Shannon this but she won't hear it. She is determined to blame him for her brother's death and storms off.

When Jack wakes up he realizes that the key to Halliburton is missing from around his neck. He wants to blame Locke, but Sayid arrives knowing the real culprit.

Jack, Kate and Sayid run through the jungle in the drenching rain and find Shannon with Locke at gunpoint.

Sayid tries to talk her down. He tells her that she can never take it back, but she won't listen. She's going to shoot him. Sayid takes his chance and tackles Shannon right as she fires the gun. Locke is only grazed, but Sayid has killed his relationship with her.

Charlie convinces Claire to give him the baby to watch so that she can get some rest. She's reluctant by finally gives in. Charlie tries everything, but can't get the baby to stop crying. Hurley tries singing James Brown to him, but that doesn't work either. Michael and Jin are working on the boat and neither are any help. Surprisingly, the baby seems to have an affinity for Sawyers voice. As long as Sawyer reads out loud, the baby is silent and happy.

Back at camp Kate tells Sayid that he just needs to give Shannon time and that he did the right thing. Sayid checks on Locke and Locke thanks him, knowing what it cost. Sayid tells him that he did it because he thinks Locke might be the key to their survival, but he doesn't trust him. And now, he's going to take him to the hatch.

Sayid Jarrah 101

Sayid has been detained in London Heathrow airport for eighteen hours by the C.I.A. and the A.S.I.S. They tell him that he's there to do them a favor. He may not be an Iraqi terrorist, but it happens that his roommate from college in Cairo is a member of a terrorist cell that has three hundred pounds of C-4. The C.I.A. wants it back. They have a bargaining chip too, they know where Nadia is and if he helps, they'll tell him where she is. They know Sayid has been looking for her.

Sayid goes to Sydney and conveniently prays at a mosque where his friend Essam prays. Essam spots him immediately and finds him when the prayers end. Essam takes him to the apartment he shares with two other guys. As Sayid has a conversation, he deftly finds a bug in the smoke detector and removes it. Essam tells his friends that Sayid was in the

Republican Guard and they wonder if it's fate that brought him there.

Sayid finds out that Essam doesn't know if his friend has procured explosives yet, but does know that he's found a martyr and it will him. Essam isn't sure if he can do it though. Sayid goes back to his contacts, but they won't let him get his friend out. He doesn't know where the C-4 is and they want the explosives. In fact, they want Sayid to convince him to go through with it. The only way to find the C-4 is for Essam to be loaded up for a target. Sayid refuses, but they remind him that they can still arrest Nadia as an enemy combatant.

Sayid convinces his friend that martyrdom is for the greater good, despite the innocents that might be killed. He tells him that the best way to serve the memory of his wife that was killed in a bombing is to make sure those responsible pay the consequences. He agrees to do the suicide bombing together.

Sayid and Essam get into a white van loaded with explosives, wearing nondescript clothes. They are given a gun in case things go awry and sent on their way. Before Essam starts the engine, Sayid tell him that he's working for the C.I.A. and that he's going to give him a ten minute lead. Essam is upset that his friend set him up and devastated when he finds out it was over a woman. He shots himself with the handgun before Sayid can stop him.

Sayid's contacts give him the information on Nadia and a ticket to Los Angeles on the next flight. She's in Irvine working in a medical testing company. Sayid's worried about his friends burial, however. No one has claimed him and they will cremate him. Sayid changes his flight so that he can claim the body and bury his friend.

Analyze This

Greater good: There is a lot of talk about the greater good in LOST. Things done for the greater good often come at a personal cost and those done selfishly at even further cost. Sayid tricks his friend onto the path of becoming a martyr for his own personal gain and pays a great cost. His decision to save Locke however, was done for the greater good. Much that Locke does, he claims he does for the greater good, but it could quite possibly be for personal gain. Jack's father said that Jack's tough upbringing was about the greater good and perhaps it will be true, but again at what cost? Is it best to do things for the greater good?

Attacking Sayid: Why did Locke really attack Sayid in the jungle? He says that he knocked him out because it was in everyone's best interest. He says that everyone was so focused on getting off the island that they weren't being reasonable. Locke feels that following the transmission would have been dangerous. Yet, isn't the hatch potentially? Why does Locke think he knows the greater good? It's possible that Locke knocked out Sayid simply because he doesn't want off the island. Whose side is Locke on, anyway?

Signs & Symbols

Revenge: Revenge is a cycle that doesn't end. In literature a character seeking revenge often takes a fatal fall from grace. Shannon's need for revenge for her brother's death could easily start an irreparable rift between the survivors.

War wounds: Both the surgery scar and the bullet graze are called war wounds on Locke. Everyone on the island wears war wounds old and new. These point to the fact that in all the survivors, a war is still raging.

Listen to What the Fans Say

Some fans speculate that the survivors are not on Earth at all, but somewhere in space. Is it possible that they have been abducted by aliens and placed in an environment that simulates their natural one, much like animals in a zoo? They may have done this in order to study humanity and see how humans thrive and interact. Being aliens they may not have gotten all the details correct. This may explain why there are polar bears on a tropical island and why the tides seem to be unnatural. This might also explain why Locke can walk and how some seem to heal incredibly quickly when wounded. Perhaps there something extra in the atmosphere that's giving the survivors a little boost?

Truth & Speculation

- Naveen's current girlfriend of six years is Barbara Hershey.

- Naveen is actually British and of Indian descent, not Middle Eastern

- In an interview with *The Honolulu Advertiser*, Naveen said of his role, "One of the biggest kicks was getting a letter from the Arab League saying how pleased they were about this. It was the first time they had seen an Arab character like that on TV."

Quotable Quips

- **Sayid** (to Melissa Cole about Nadia): Nobody calls her Noor.

- **Shannon** (to Sayid): John Locke killed my brother. Will you do something about that?

- **Locke** (to Sayid): Jack called me a liar in fornt of every man, woman and child I've come to know over the past month. And maybe there's a part of you that thinks maybe there isn't a plane out here at all.

- **Hurley** (To Charlie after singing James Brown to the baby): Dude, that's all I got.

- **Locke** (to Sayid): You were hit from behind, knocked unconscious. When you woke up, the transceiver, your equipment was destroyed. That was me.

- **Charlie** (Asking Sawyer to say something): Okay, fine. I liked that thing a lot better inside than I like it outside.

Sawyerisms
About Aaron: Baby Huey

To Charlie: Chuckie

Seven Degrees of LOST

Nadia works in Irvine California the same city **Locke** works in.

Sayid ended up on Flight 815 because he changed his flight to bury his friend.

Episode Twenty-Two: Born to Run

Summary

Charlie points out to Kate that when they are rescued they will all be incredibly famous. He's banking on it for the record sales, but Kate looks worried. She's even more concerned when Leslie Arzt, one of the other survivors points out that the monsoon season is starting and the raft needs to launched immediately. Michael's not sure if he's right, but doesn't want to risk it.

Kate starts jockeying for a position on the raft, but they're all filled. Sawyer has still got a spot and Jin is definitely going. Kate tries to convince Michael that she's the better candidate because she has sailing experience. When Kate tries to suggest that Michael shouldn't take Walt, she steps over the line and Michael ends the discussion.

When Sawyer makes a dumb comment about why they are bringing salted fish on the raft, Michael starts to think over Kate's proposition. Sawyer obviously knows nothing about sailing. Sawyer isn't happy about the idea of being replaced by Kate and confronts her. He knows she was the Marshal's prisoner and wants a clean escape. He's not giving up his spot though. Kate tells him that she wants it, she'll take it.

Sayid brings Jack into the jungle to look at the hatch. Locke insisted he be brought. Jack takes a look at it and wants to figure out a way to open it. It might have supplies or work as a shelter. Sayid is not pleased. He thinks they should re-bury it.

Meanwhile, Michael gets sick from some water that he drank and everyone starts pointing fingers. Sawyer and Kate are both possibilities. Sawyer spills the beans to everyone that Kate is a convict on the run and has every reason to want on the raft. No mention what she might be willing to do to get there. He pulls the passport of the drowned woman out of Kate's backpack to prove it. Kate swears that she didn't poison Michael, but the damage is already done.

Walt comes to Locke to tell him that he didn't poison his father. Locke already knows this and wouldn't tell on him anyway. Walt came to tell him something more important though. He tells him not to open that thing and leaves without explaining further.

Jack approaches Sun and asks her why she did it, why she tried to poison her husband and accidentally poisoned Michael. Sun only wanted him to stay, doesn't want him to die out at sea. Jack understands and won't let anyone know it was her, but tells her that he's going and she should say goodbye. Later, Sun tells Kate that Jack knows, but that she didn't tell him it was Kate's idea.

Preparations for setting sail continue and Walt confesses to his father that is was him that set fire to the first boat. He didn't want to leave. Rather than being angry, Michael offers that they can stay, but Walt has changed his mind. He is adamant that they leave.

Kate Austen 101

A blonde woman sneaks into a recently vacated motel room and dyes her hair. As she turns in the shower, we see that it's Kate. She retrieves a letter that's waiting for her at the desk and it's not good news. Her mother is dying of cancer.

Kate goes to the hospital where her mother is staying, pretending to have a flower delivery, but when she sees the guard outside her door, she keeps walking. She hides in Tom Brendon's car instead. He's surprised to see her, but happy. Kate asks for his help.

Back at Tom's house, Kate looks at the photos on his refrigerator. He's got two children that are away with his wife at his in-laws house. They've got some time to kill while they wait for the MRI that Tom has set up for her mother. Kate wants to go dig up a time capsule that they buried as kids.

They have a beer and dig it up, a bunch of knick knack including a toy plane and a cassette tape inside. In the car they listen to tape, revealing that they were childhood sweethearts. Tom put the plane in because it was given to him for flying alone to Dallas and was important to him. From little Katie's part of the tape it sounds as though she has always wanted to run away and hints that there's a good reason. Reminiscing, they kiss, but quickly pull away.

Back at the hospital, Tom leaves Kate alone in the MRI room with her mother. She tries to say hello to her, but her mother immediately starts screaming for help and doesn't stop. Her calls bring a security guard and Kate knocks him out before he can call for help. Kate takes Tom's keys and runs. Tom follows her and jumps in his car with her. A state trooper blocks the exit of the parking garage.

The trooper gets out and pulls his gun. Kate tells Tom to get out, but he won't leave. He wants her to give herself up. When he doesn't get out when she demands it once more, she drives right into the state trooper's car. He fires three shots at Kate's vehicle and she keeps going until she hits another car. She turns to check on Tom, but he's taken a bullet to the chest and is already dead. Kate leaves him and runs.

Analyze This

Withholding Information: Both Locke and Jack choose to give and withhold information as they see fit for the group as a whole. Jack has kept Kate's past and the stronghold of guns to himself and Locke has kept the hatch a secret. Is either justified in their decisions? Perhaps it is just that neither thoroughly saw themselves as leaders. Now that all the information is on the table, will Jack and Locke be able to work as a team?

Walt and the Hatch: Why does Walt know about the hatch and what does he know about it? Even if he overheard Locke and Boone, he couldn't possibly know that it is dangerous. No one has discovered what's inside. Although Walt was so determined to stay on the island that he was willing to set fire to the raft, now he seems determined to leave. What does Walt know that no one does?

Signs & Symbols

Poison: In literature the use of poison to change fate is often met with a bad ending. Romeo and Juliet died star-crossed lovers due to a misunderstanding over poison. Suggested by Kate the tactic ultimately didn't work out for her or Sun.

Confession: The act of confession is an important facet of LOST. Walt confesses to his father as if to cleanse himself before the journey. Jack eases a confession out of Jin that she poisoned her husband. It seems important the everyone fact their sins on this island both past and present before they can move on.

Tom Brendon: Kate's childhood sweetheart is a foil to her now. He demonstrates all of the things that Kate could have had were she not on the run. Kate will most likely never have a family and life of comfort like his. The foil is even further elevated when he dies.

Listen to What the Fans Say

It has been suggested that perhaps LOST itself is a backgammon game, mirroring the small games played by the survivors. Perhaps the survivors are all "pieces" in a game being played by two invisible opponents. The Lostaways represent one player and the Others represent that player's opponent. If this is true the whispers on the island could be the players or even spectators that are watching the game. Backgammon is the oldest game known to humankind, so perhaps it is being utilized in some sort of high stakes competition. Perhaps it is actually a battle of good versus evil just as Locke presented it at the beginning of the series. Proponents of this theory point out that Louis Carroll wrote Alice in Wonderland as a chess game that ends when the pawn Alice is crowned queen. So maybe the writers are following a similar experiment with backgammon.

Truth & Speculation

- David Fury said in an interview with SciFi.com that "the island has been around for millennia, many people have found themselves on it and as far as we know, nobody has ever gotten off."

- There was a line cut from an episode with Rousseau where she is asked what they were studying and she says, "time."

- According to an article in USA Today, the writers are determined to avoid an "X-Files" scenario in which the mythology of the show becomes too complicated for viewers to follow and never gets adequately described.

Quotable Quips

- **Charlie** (to Kate): They built a sodding boat. And when they get picked up, the helicopters will come, making us ridiculously and eternally famous.

- **Sawyer** (to Kate): Don't give me the "aw, golly" eyes. Michael told me you were jockeying for my spot on the raft.

- **Locke** (to Jack): How long did you have that case full of guns before you decided the rest of us needed to know? You used your best discretion; I used mine.

- **Hurley** (about Michael and Jin): Well, they fight like a married couple building a raft together.

- **Walt** (to Locke): Don't open it, Mr. Locke. Don't open that thing.

Sawyerisms

To Michael: Boss

To Michael: Captain

About Arzt: Damn High School Science Teacher

To Michael: Mikey

To Kate: Puddin'

To Jin: Sulu

To Kate: Sweetcheeks

Seven Degrees of LOST

Kate's childhood sweetheart was **Tom Brennan**
The **toy airplane** belonged to **Tom Brendon**
Kate's mother is **Diane Jansen**

Episode Twenty-Three: Exodus (1)

Summary

The rest of the camp on the beach is sleeping and Walt gets up to relieve himself. Danielle Rousseau appears from the jungle, a rifle strapped over her shoulder and heads into the camp. Walt calls for her gather to wake up. Michael gets up and tries to stop her, but she finds Sayid. He calms everyone down and asks Danielle why she's there. Danielle tells him that the others are coming. She explains that the last time they appeared it was after she saw a pillar of black smoke and they came and took her baby, Alex. Now they are coming again and everyone must run or hide.

Jack is not necessarily convinced that Danielle isn't crazy, but Locke points out that it still may be true. Michael trying to get off the island, but still has a lot of work to do on the boat. Jack gathers the troops hoping to get the boat finished and out to sea. Using palm logs as rails, everyone gathers, pulling the boat onto the logs and moving it toward the water. Then the boat gets too much momentum and slides of the rails and hitting the sand, the impact breaking the mast. Michael blames Sawyer. While they argue something catches their eye and makes them stop. In the distance a pillar of black smoke rises from the jungle.

Jack and Locke realize the only safety may be the hatch, but still they're unsure how to open it. Danielle tells them that they can find dynamite at the Black Rock. Artz hears of their plan and insists on coming along. Dynamite sitting that long in the jungle is dangerous and he thinks he may be the only one that can manage it. He's coming along.

By the time they get back from the Black Rock, the boat will already be gone, so Jack says his good byes. He gives Sawyer one of the guns, just in case. And Sawyer at last tells Jack the story of meeting his father in the bar. He lets him know that his father was proud of him. Charlie gathers messages to send in a bottle with the sailors. Hurley and Kate say their good byes, but Sawyer is no where to be found.

Danielle leads Jack, Kate, Arzt, Locke and Hurley into the Dark Territory. When they get close to the Black Rock, she makes a comment about her crew getting sick and Montand losing his arm there. Arzt decides this isn't the trip for him and is turning back. They let him go and continue, but it isn't long before he comes running back screaming, the monster behind him.

Locke stops Hurley and they both stand still. Danielle pulls the others into the trees to hide. The creature heads the other way. Kate asks Danielle what it is and she states that it's a security system. It protects the island. The team walks further and Danielle stops them. They are at the Black Rock. Everyone looks up in wonder at an old ship, somehow stranded miles inland.

Walt leaves Shannon with Vincent, telling her that he can protect her. Perhaps more important, he has good ear. He listened well when Walt's mom died. If Shannon wants to talk about Boone, he'll listen to her as well. Shannon tears up and agrees to take him, but only until they are rescued.

Sayid has pieced together a sort of radar for the boat and found a flare on the Beechcraft. He suggests that they use it wisely. There's only the one. Sawyer has created a perfect mast to replace that one that was broken. Meanwhile Sun gives Jin and English/Korean dictionary she has made of words that might be important on the trip. He is touched and begins to cry. He's only leaving because he thinks he's being punished for how he has treated her. He has to go to try and save them.

With everyone's help, the raft is pushed out into the ocean and floats away. Vincent tries to follow, but Walt sends him back to Shannon. The survivors wave and cheer as their hope is carried out to sea.

Flight 815 Boarding Call 101

Michael and Walt are in a hotel room in Sydney before the flight. It's obvious that it's the last place that Walt wants to be. He deliberately infuriating Michael, turning up the television and refusing to turn it down. Then he grabs his dog and tries to run off. Michael corners him in the hallway and Walt makes a scene. He screams that he's not going, that Michael is not his father.

Jack has a drink at the airport bar and meets Ana Lucia, who asks what he was yelling at the girl at the check-in counter by introduction. She says she's on his flight and is sorry that his father died. She asks if he's married and he tells that he's not anymore. She's in seat 42-F and asks Jack if he wants to trade. Then she gets a call and promises to have a drink with him on the plane.

Sawyer is in a police station being harassed by Calderwood. Seems Sawyer was in bar fight the night before and head-butted the Minister of Agriculture, Fisheries and Forestry. They've run his file and discovered that his name is James Ford, con man extraordinaire and Calderwood is not pleased to have him in his country. He has a ticket for Sawyer on Flight 815 and he's never to set foot in Australia again.

Kate is in the backroom of the Sydney airport with the Marshall who is checking his Halliburton. The airport official asks why he has five guns. He asks Kate if she would like to answer for him. She doesn't. The official also wonders about the toy plane. When she still keeps her mouth shut, he explains that it belonged to her childhood sweetheart who she got killed while she was on the run. At some point Kate started to call him at home, telling him she had mitigating circumstances. He thinks she was taunting him. He continues to talk, mocking Kate until she lashes out and pins him to the wall. The marshal elbows her and explains that that's why he needs five guns.

Shannon sits doing a word puzzle, waiting for her flight. Sayid comes up and asks if she'll watch his bag for a minute. She barely looks and says sure noncommittally. Boone comes back and tells her that he couldn't get them into first class. She's irritated and wants him to try again. Boone and her bicker and Shannon tells him that he is no idea what she is capable of doing. She stops a security guard and tells him that an Arab guy just left his bags and walked away.

Sun brings Jin some coffee and a snack. She puts a napkin in his lap and arranges their food. A woman at a nearby table comments to her husband, disgusted by Sun fawning over her husband. Sun can hear and understands. When Sun puts food in front of Jin she knocks over his coffee on onto him. She tries to dab it off and Jin looks around for a restroom and leaves. The woman comments that it's so "Memoirs of a Geisha," still thinking Sun can't understands her.

Analyze This

Flashbacks: The flashbacks in this episode demonstrate how far the relationships have changed and grown since the survivors of flight 815 were stranded. Jin and Sun's conversation mirrors the pain of knowing English, while everyone around you thinks you don't understand. Now we know that she is free to communicate. We also understand her relationship with Jin and know that much of his posturing isn't disrespectful, but cultural and often loving. These flashbacks bring us back to the beginning and the first season full circle. Where will the next season take the survivors?

Sawyer's Atonement: Just like Walt confesses in the last episode, Sawyer seems to be cleansing himself as well. He at last tells Jack about meeting his father in the bar in Sydney. Although he has done nothing to help build the raft the entire time it was being built, he at last puts his back into making the mast, a crucial piece of the ship. The only thing he didn't get to do was say good bye to Kate and he looked for her before they sailed. Is he slate clean enough that he will get to the next place in the journey?

Signs & Symbols

Vincent: Dogs are the symbol of faithfulness, courage and guardianship. By leaving Vincent with Shannon he leaves her with all that she lost when her brother died.

Message in a bottle: The messages in a bottle symbolize hope and support. The survivors send their messages across the sea and also send their support and prayers with the sailors.

Dictionary: Sun's gift of a dictionary stands for everything that has not or could not be said between the two of them. By giving Jin the English language, Sun eliminates the one barrier between them. At last Jin opens up and tells her why he has been silent.

Listen to What the Fans Say

The writers of LOST have expressed their admiration of writer Michael Crichton, who often mixes science fiction with science fact to create a more believable and compelling story. Fans have wondered if this means that writers have used a little something from Crichton's book Prey. In the book the government has been working on creating nanobots, robots the size of dust particles. They are invisible but when swarming together look like dust, or perhaps black smoke. Nanobots can heal humans or destroy them, carrying them off or entering them and causing them harm. Could this explain the "monster" and how Locke could suddenly walk? It might even explain the sickness of Rousseau's team. Perhaps the nanobots have become sentient and have gotten out of control, which would explain the island's abandonment expect for hapless castaways. It could also be a scientific explanation for everything on the island.

Truth & Speculation

- Naveen Andrews and Terry O'Quinn both received Emmy nominations for Supporting Actor in a drama series

- In Douglas Adams' book "Hitchhiker's Guide to the Galaxy," the number 42 is the answer to life, the universe and everything.

- LOST is rumored to be the most expensive pilot ever produced.

Quotable Quips

- **Danielle** (about the black smoke): The others. You have only three choices. Run...hide...or die.
- **Arzt** (about the dynamite): You want to keep a secret, don't tell the fat guy.
- **Arzt** (to Jack): God knows how long that dynamite has been out there. And From what I can tell, Madame Nutso doesn't seem too concerned how to handle it. So unless you want to blow up, I'm coming with you.
- **Hurley** (to Arzt about his name): I remember it from the plane's manifest. I think Leslie's a bitchin' name.
- **Arzt** (about the Black Rock): Yeah, I wanted to help, but that was before Montand lost his frickin' arm.

Sawyerisms

To Calderwood: Doctor

Seven Degrees of LOST

Jack meets **Ana Lucia** in the airport bar.
Shannon has **Sayid** detained at the airport.

Episode Twenty-Four: Exodus (2)

(Two-Hour Season Finale)

Summary

Claire is having trouble getting her baby to settle and everybody is leaving the beach for the caves. Charlie tries to help her and she gets upset. Charlie is really worried and asks Sayid for a gun. Sayid refuses and tells Charlie that he's too emotionally involved. The best thing Charlie can do is help Claire pack and move.

Shannon is struggling to bring the dog and a ton of luggage to the caves. Sayid realizes that she is bringing her brother's luggage as well. She is falling apart. Everything is too much. Sayid cups her face in his hand and tells her that it won't be too much if he carries it for her.

Danielle leaves the group at the Black Rock. Locke tells Jack to let her go, he can lead them back from there. They go inside and discover that the Black Rock was a slave ship, the skeletons slaves still chained inside the hull. They find the dynamite and decide to bring it out rather than trying to pry it open. Once they get outside, Artz has fit. They should be moving it. He has them put down box and move away. He explains that the dynamite sweats nitroglycerin in the head and they need to pull them out individually and wrap them in wet cloth. Artz does this with the first piece, lecturing the whole time, apparently not paying close enough attention because the stick in his hand explodes.

Hurley is pretty shook up by the whole ordeal, but everyone else is ready for plan B. Locke packs the driest dynamite he can find in wet shirts and they split it into two backpacks. Kate demands that she gets to carry one and Jack argues with her that he should be the one. They agree to draw straws and Kate wins. Staggering out, they head for the hatch.

Charlie and Claire are preparing to head to the caves. Charlie has made her a sling to carry the baby in and she's grateful. Then Rousseau shows up looking of Sayid. She seems hysterical. Charlie goes to get him and leaves Claire alone with her. As soon as he's gone, Rousseau asks to hold the baby. Claire is uncomfortable and then she notices the scratch marks on Rousseau's arm and remembers. She asks, "why did I scratch you?" a terrified look on her face.

When Charlie returns with Sayid, Rousseau is gone and Claire has been hit on the head, her baby taken. Charlie is furious and punches Sayid. He grabs Charlie by his throat and holds him off. Fighting will get them nowhere and Sayid knows where Rousseau is going. She's headed to the black smoke to make a trade with the others. She's hoping to get her own child back. Claire wants to come, but Charlie calms her down and promises that she will bring her baby back to her.

Out on the ocean the sailors are getting a view of how big the island is and it seems huge. Michael shows Walt how the transmitter and the radar work. Michael lets Walt drive the boat. Michael explains that they're heading north by north east. Then Walt asks his dad what happened with him and his mother and why he never saw him. When Michael tells Walt that his mother thought it was best for him, Walt tells him that she was wrong. Then suddenly the boat lurches.

Jin shouts "rudder," they've lost it. Michael's yelling to stop the boat and Sawyer jumps in after it. Jin brings down the sails and Michael throws him a rope. They pull him in with the rudder, a close call. When Michael hands Sawyer back his shirt and feels the gun wrapped inside, he's not pleased.

On the way to the black smoke, Charlie and Sayid stop to rest a moment by the Beechcraft. Sayid tells him about the drugs and Charlie sees the broken statue and the heroine. He stares at the drugs. They move along and Charlie stumbles into on of Rousseau's traps. He has a huge gouge in his forehead. Sayid tells him to go back, but Charlie begs him to do some sort of field dressing so he can continue. Sayid agrees, noting Charlie isn't going to like it. He opens a bullet, covers the wound with gun powder and lights it on fire. Painful, but it staunches the bleeding.

Gingerly walking in the direction of the hatch, Kate, Hurley, Jack and Locke hear a familiar sound. Everyone puts down their back pack and runs, except for Locke who seems intent on playing chicken with the security system. He steps toward it instead of away. A tree is pulled up by the roots next to him. Locke looks up into the creature and this time what he sees terrifies him. He runs. Something catches him by the ankle and drags him across the jungle floor. There's a clicking noise like gears. Jack jumps on Locke and whatever is pulling Locke, easily pulls them both along. Then a hole opens up and Locke is going down it. The only thing that stops him is Jack at the edge, pulling him back up.

Locke tells Jack to let him go. Jack yells at Kate to get him a stick of dynamite and that it's in his backpack not hers. He tells her to throw it in the hole, he can't hold Locke any longer. Locke tells her not to do it, but Kate listens to Jack.

Out of the explosion a cloud of dark smoke rises from the hole. It seems to flee with intent.

Jack confronts Locke about his behavior and Locke insists it was a test of the island, that nothing was going to kill him. Locke thinks that everyone arrived on the island because it was their destiny. This theory does nothing for Jack.

Back at the hatch Kate runs a fuse while Hurley plants the dynamite and Jack and Locke rig the charges. Kate confronts Jack about switching backpacks and Jack tells her that if people want him to be a leader then they are going to have to accept his decisions. He needs to know if she is in his camp because if they survive the night he thinks they are going to have a Locke problem.

Everyone is set to detonate when Hurley sees the numbers on the hatch. He starts to yell, "stop!" He tells them that the numbers are bad that they can't do this. It's too late though, Locke is lighting the fuse. Hurley tries to stamp out the fuse, but it's not working. Jack tackles him just as the dynamite explodes.

Charlie and Sayid find the fire. It's a burning tire, but if there were people there, they are gone now. They find Rousseau and the baby as well. Rousseau is distraught. She hear the others whispering that they were coming for the boy and thought they meant Claire's baby. Charlie is furious with the woman, but Sayid pities her. They take the baby back to Claire.

On the boat, Michael tries to give back Jin his watch. Jin looks at it long and hard and then gives it back to Michael, a gift. Later Michael and Sawyer discuss why Sawyer's on the raft. Then something pops up on the radar. They think it might be a ship, but aren't certain. There's only one flare so they can't take any chances. Just as the blip disappears off the radar they shoot the gun, and whatever it is turns back.

A boat rumbles up, a flood light flashing and they think they're saved, already rejoicing. A bearded asks their story and seems happy to be saving them, until he says something that stops the revelry. He's going to have to take the boy. The floodlight goes out, two men from the other boat grab Walt. Sawyer pulls his gun, but is shot before he can pull the trigger and falls into the ocean. Jin dives in after him. A woman from the boat throws a Molotov cocktail and the raft bursts into flames. The boat of strangers pulls away with Walt, screaming for his dad.

At the hatch, the cover has definitely taken some damage. Locke and Jack are able to just push it aside. There's a metal ladder on one side of passage that seems to deep into the earth.

Flight 815 Boarding 101

We see Jin and Sun in the airport again, this time from Jin's point of view. Sun spills coffee on Jin and he heads to the bathroom. In the background Sayid is being escorted by two security officers who are letting him go. In the restroom, a Caucasian man in a Hawaiian shirt starts a conversation with him in English and then converts to Korean. He continues his conversation saying that he works for Mr. Paik. They know that Jin is planning to run away and if he tries it, he will lose his wife. He is not free and never has been.

Charlie is in a hotel room, trying to get his bags together. His flight leaves in a couple of hours. There's a blonde woman in the room with him, wearing a t-shirt and black underwear. She asks him if she can get one more "bump" for the road. He tells her it's all gone and she doesn't believe him. He thinks she's a fan and offers to leave him with a CD, but she doesn't even know who his band is. She just wants the drugs. They get into a wrestling match over the drugs he has in his hand, but she doesn't manage to get them away from him.

Michael sits with Walt in the airport. Walt is playing with his hand held game and completely ignoring him. Michael gets up to make a phone call, telling Walt he has to check in at work. He calls his mother instead. He's going to need help. He leaves for work at 5 am and doesn't know how he'll get

Walt to school. He wants his mom to take his son, but she is refusing. He yells that he wasn't supposed to be his, that this wasn't part of the plan, but he's getting no where. He hangs up the phone to see Walt standing next to him. Walt tells him he needs new batteries.

Hurley wakes up in his hotel room in Sydney and the power is off and he's late. He can't miss his flight. His mother's birthday is the next day. The elevator is packed, his car breaks down, the ticket agent is painfully slow, then she makes him purchase another ticket because of his size, and the terminal is at the other side of the airport. Hurley races through the airport, waits in line at the security checkpoint, pays an old man on a scooter $1600 to let him use it and just makes it to the gate just as the jet way closes. He begs the attendant to let him on and she agrees, noting that it's his lucky day.

The airline attendants can't find the chairs used to load disabled persons on to the plane. Locke can either take another plane or have the attendants help him on. They have to carry him on, much to his embarrassment.

As all the other passengers board there are quick glimpses of them interacting or ignoring one another. All sixteen major players are accounted for, including Hurley who boards last and settles in to put on his headphones and read his Green Lantern/Flash: Faster Friends #1 comic book.

Analyze This

LOST: The name LOST is a perfect one for the show, full of many meanings that are different for each of the characters. The obvious is that they are lost on a deserted island, but each is lost in their own way. They've lost heart, hope, family, freedom and all are striving to regain them. Will they always be lost or will each character discover how to be found?

Locke Problems: What does Jack mean when he says if they survive the night they are going to have Locke problems? Does Jack think the other man has gone crazy? Or is it just that Jack is finally ready to step up to being leader and his philosophies are too different from Locke's? Perhaps Locke is thinking the same thing, but he's been strategizing since he arrived on the island. If someone has to win, who will be the better man?

Signs & Symbols

This is your lucky day: When said to Hurley when he makes it on the plane, this is a perfect example of irony.

Luggage: Everyone has brought physical luggage on the island, but some of it symbolizes the emotional luggage they have brought along or gather while they've been there. Shannon carrying Boone's luggage demonstrates that she is not ready to move on.

Steering the boat: When Michael finally lets Walt steer the boat he treats him more like an adult than a child. This is the first time he's let Walt take control of the rudder. As the boy begins to feel like he has more control over his life, he open up more to his father.

Listen to What the Fans Say

Is it possible that there is something extraordinary about Vincent the dog? Walt seems to have a connection with animals albeit not necessarily a kind one. He may have conjured up the polar bears and caused the Australian bird to kill itself. Vincent has been a constant on the island and seems to often appear at pivotal moments. Vincent is the first thing that Jack sees when he wakes from the crash. He was spotted on the hike to higher ground with the transceiver. The dog somehow survives the polar bears and "lostzilla" not to mention the plane crash unscathed. He has been Walt's nearly constant companion, but a welcome gift to Shannon after her brother's death. If Walt is indeed "special" he could certainly have imbued some of this into a dog that is loved so dearly. Many fans speculate that Vincent may play a more important role that what is obvious.

Truth & Speculation

- The writers originally wanted to reveal some part of the island mythology through the eyes of Vincent the dog, but this idea leaked and the writers scrapped it.

- Harold Perrineau can't swim and since the first season finale has taken swimming lessons.

- According to the writers, when the viewers know what the island is then the show will be over.

Quotable Quips

- **Charlie** (to Sayid about wanting a gun): I killed a murderer. I did us all a favor.

- **Rousseau** (to Hurley about the Black Rock): Are you on the same island I am?

- **Artz** (to Hurley): I know a clique when I see one. I teach high school, pally.

LOST: ULTIMATE UNOFFICIAL GUIDE

- **Michael** (to Sawyer about the gun in his shirt): Here's your shirt. You should put it on before you burn.

- **Locke** (to Hurley): I like Twinkies too.

- **Hurley**: Whoever named this place "dark territory"...genius.

- **Hurley** (to the airline attendant): Please. For the love of all that is good and holy in the world, let me on this plane.

- **Hurley** (at the hatch): Can I have a flashlight? Cause, uh, the torch around the dynamite thing...not making a whole lot of sense to me.

- **Sawyer** (on the raft): Hey Han, you and Chewie want to slow down a second and talk to me here. We have to fire the flare.

Sawyerisms

To Walt: Kazoo

To Jin: Chewie

To Michael: Han

Seven Degrees of LOST

Charlie and **Hurley** were in the same hotel in Sydney.
Sayid passes behind **Jin** in the airport.

Cool Extras

Literary and Film/TV References and Parallels

Literature

The Bridge of San Luis Rey, by Thornton Wilder
Watership Down, by Richard Adams
A Wrinkle In Time, by Madeleine L'Engle
Lord of the Flies, by William Golding
Hitchhiker's Guide to the Galaxy, by Douglas Adams
Heart of Darkness, by Joseph Conrad
The Stand by Stephen King
Other Stephen King Homages
 Carrie
 Storm of the Century
 The Langoliers
 The Tommyknockers
Alice in Wonderland by Lewis Carroll
Shakespeare
 Othello
 The Tempest
 The Taming of the Shrew
Nietzsche
Jane Austen

Film

The Fugitive (TR)
Rosemary's Baby (RBA)
Lord of the Rings (COWBOY)
Indiana Jones (NUM)
Apocolypse Now (NUM)
Star Wars (Special, Exodus 1, Exodus 2)
Finding Nemo (Whatever the Case May Be)
Ghostbusters (RBA)

Willie Wonka and The Little Princess (WALK)
Citizen Kane (Numbers)
Office Space (WALK)
Hitchcock's Psycho (BTR)
Jacob's Ladder (Exodus 3)

Television

The Office (HOME)
Star Trek (COWBOY)
Fantasy Island (COWBOY)
Survivor (BTR)

The Numbers – 4, 8, 15, 16, 23, 42

Although the writers have expressed that 23 is the most important number thematically in LOST, they have had a great deal of fun inserting all the winning lottery number in various instances. Of course, the fans have had even more fun discovering them and have found many that are unintentional.

FOUR

- There are FOUR scratches on Jack's face in the pilot.
- For FOUR years Locke was in his wheelchair.
- There are FOUR guns in the marshal's case.
- There FOUR aces on Boone's t shirt.
- FOUR days pass before the survivors burn the fuselage.
- It will take FOUR people to help dig Jack out of the cave in.
- Boone brought FOUR refills for Shannon's inhaler.
- It's been FOUR years since Sawyer made his "birthday wish".
- FOUR people will fit on Michael's raft.
- It's been FOUR years since Hurley's grandfather got his pacemaker.
- For FOUR months Michelangelo stared at marble before he began to carve.
- The nurse taking care of Michael has FOUR kids.
- Boones asks if they are going to stare at the hatch for FOUR months.
- Locke ties up Boone FOUR miles due west of camp.
- Locke sets FOUR traps around camp to catch Ethan.
- Hurley says Charlie shot Ethan four times.
- It's been FOUR years since Sam Toome killed himself.

- The psychic spent FOUR months trying to convince Claire to raise her baby alone.
- There are FOUR Oceanic planes on the mobile in Claire's dream.
- There are FOUR dotted dice in a backgammon game.
- Locke says to Boone that FOUR he wouldn't have believed his crazy talk either
- The number FOUR on Sarah's t shirt in Do No Harm.
- Jack's dad's watch had the minute hand on FOUR.
- Jack plays the key B4 on the piano.
- Shannon asks Boone what he and Locke have been doing in the jungle for the past FOUR days.
- Sayid said the French signal could be a SAT 4.
- Leonard was playing the game Connect FOUR.
- Walt says he needs to roll a FOUR and a three in the backgammon game.
- Plane hit turbulence at 40,000 feet.
- Charlie jokes about Locke bringing 400 knives.
- Adam and Eve" have been in the caves for 40 years.
- In White Rabbit, Locke's watch's minute hand is set to FOUR.
- The types of explosives stolen were C4.
- The magazine Sawyer reads says the car has 400 horsepower.
- The magazine says the car has a 4.4 liter power plant under the hood.
- Mr. Arzt says it will be FOUR months before the next time they can launch the raft.
- Shannon asks Boone what's a FOUR letter word for "I don't care"
- There are FOUR scratches on Danielle's arm from Claire.
- FOUR people kidnap Walt.
- In The Pilot the clock inside of the cockpit displays 4:00.

- Jack says it has to be almost 4:00 when Kate, Locke and Boone are out look for Claire.
- The dice read FOUR in Deus Ex Machina when the camera focuses on the Mouse Trap board.

EIGHT

- Claire was EIGHT months pregnant when they crashed.
- The hit man tells Jin to drive EIGHT kilometers.
- EIGHT people die in Hurley's shoe factory fire.
- There are EIGHT whiskey shots between Sawyer and Christian Shepherd.
- Kate would spend EIGHT hours at a time in the woods with her father tracking deer.
- It's been EIGHT years since Michael got hit by car.
- Locke and Helen have been talking for EIGHT months.
- Charlie went without his guitar for EIGHT days.
- In EIGHT weeks Drive Shaft was going to tour.
- EIGHT days after the crash Jack and some of the survivors move to the caves.
- Michael worked in construction for EIGHT years.
- It had been EIGHT months since farmer's wife died when he met Kate.
- Boone's shirt has the Chinese symbol for EIGHT.
- Jack's best man says he should have had EIGHT beers before giving his toast.
- Sawyer's was EIGHT when his dad killed himself and his wife.
- Shannon was EIGHT when her dad married Boone's mom.
- News station that interviewed Hurley was channel 8.

- Claire was missing for EIGHT days since Ethan took her.
- In the Pilot Part 2 when Charlie takes off his shoe, inside it says size EIGHT.
- The number EIGHT appears in Locke's license plate.
- The EIGHT ball is on the pool table in Confidence Man.
- Sayid was kept for 18 hours in the holding cell.
- The magazine Sawyer reads says the car has a V8 engine.
- Hurley says Twinkies stay fresh for 8,000 years.
- The guy on the scooter that Hurley approaches has crazy 8's written on his hat.
- Kate's mother's room was number 208.
- EIGHT is the number on the bottle of hair dye that Kate uses in Born To Run.

FIFTEEN

- There are FIFTEEN members on Danielle's research team.
- The number FIFTEEN is on the whiskey bottle from which Sawyer and Christian drink.
- Boone says he spent FIFTEEN hours on a plane to come rescue his sister.
- There are FIFTEEN kilometers to nearest town from the Australian farm.
- Sun was supposed to leave the airport at 11:15.
- Randy tells Locke he needs the reports in by noon, not 12:15.
- Shannon says she doesn't want to sit near a crying baby for the next 15 hours.

- The attendant in the airport looks up the information for Hurley's flight. On the computer screen it says the departure time is 14:15.
- Michael tells Sawyer the raft is 15 miles offshore.
- The Colorado license plate in Kate's trunk, shown in Born To Run, was NUR 153.
- Sayid's watch reads 10:15 when he gives Michael the plane's radar emitter in Exodus Part 1.
- Sun's watch reads 11:15 when giving Jin the list of English words spelled out phonetically in Exodus Part 1.

SIXTEEN

- Danielle's distress signal has been looping for SIXTEEN years.
- When Hurley won the lottery, no one has won for SIXTEEN weeks.
- It's been SIXTEEN years since Sam and Lenny first heard the numbers.
- The number SIXTEEEN shows on the numerical die in the backgammon game.
- Jack, Kate, and Charlie found the pilot SIXTEEN hours after the crash.
- Jack's first solo operation was on a SIXTEEN year old.
- Jack told the lady at the airport desk he had to land in LAX in SIXTEEN hours to bury his father.
- Sawyer tired to scam $160,000.
- There is a poster on the wall of the pool hall in Confidence Man, the date is June 16th.
- It's been SIXTEEN years since Kate and Tom buried the time capsule until she took the flight.
- Sawyer was reads a note form the bottle that Hugo left his mom 160 million dollars.

- Hurley pays the guy on the scooter $1,600 dollars for it.

TWENTY-THREE

- TWENTY-THREE is the number that appears on the waist measure that the tuxedo guy has around his neck.
- The reward for turning Kate in is $23,000.
- The digits 23 appear as part of a pin number on one of the crates found inside the drug plane.
- The digits 23 appear on the license plate that hit Locke in Deus Ex Machina.
- When Michael gives Jin the watch back in House Of The Rising Sun, the minute hand is on 23.
- The watch on Jack's wrist when signing papers in All The Best Cowboys Have Daddy Issues has the minute hand on 23.
- The watch on Sun's father's wrist when signing a paper in ...In Translation has the minute hand on 23.
- Drive Shaft is # 234 on the jukebox.
- There is a poster of the wall at the pool hall in Confidence Man, the date is May 23rd.
- When Michael looks at the clock in the hotel room it displays 5:23 AM.
- Jack's seat number was 23B.
  When Claire's baby is taken the time on Charlie's watch is 7:23 PM.
- Hurley's hotel room was on floor 23.
- Hurley looks up at a sign in the airport that says gates 14 thru 23.
- Hurley's flight took off from gate 23.
- Michael and Walt were sitting in row 23 on the airplane.

- In Deus Ex Machina when the camera focuses on the Mouse Trap game, at the moment the mouse is being caught you can see the numbers 23 on two different sides of the board.

FOURTY-TWO

- There are FOURTY-TWO spaces on a game of Connect Four.
- The book number 742 appears behind the husband looking to adopt Claire's baby in Raised By Another.
- The nurse who talks to Michael in Special is wearing a watch, the minute hand is on 42.
- Sayid's watch in the Pilot Part 2 has it's minute hand set on 42.
- Ana's seat number was 42F.
- The lady at the desk in the airport looks up in the information for Hurley's flight -- On the computer screen it says the arrival time in Los Angeles will be 10:42.
- In Born To Run when the camera focuses on Joanna's passport we see 42.

815

- The safety deposit box that held the toy airplane was 815..
- Oceanic flight # 815.
- The copier's Charlie was trying to sell were model # C 815.
- When Claire had her dream about the baby being taken, the flight number of the plane hanging from the mobile was 815.
- Sayid is walking by a building in The Greater Good. The building has the numbers 815 on the door.

- Kate and Tom buried the time capsule on August 15 1989. (8/15).
- In Born To Run, after Tom is shot the camera focuses in on the toy plane. Near the toy plane we can see a baseball with the numbers 815 written on it.

ALL NUMBERS
- Hurleys Lotto Numbers
- The soccer players Hurley runs by in the airport wear these numbers on their shirts.
- Numbers on the hatch
- The numbers on Desmond's injection

Find your seat on Oceanic Flight 815

- Go to the "official" Oceanic Airlines Website. http://www.oceanic air.com/
- At the bottom, where it says "Travelers," enter Hurley's unlucky lottery numbers: 4, 8, 15, 16, 23 and 42.
- Click the "Find" button.
- Click on the row numbers on the flight's seating chart that match Hurley's numbers.

Some Easter Eggs on the DVDs

Lost Season One Distress Call:

Go into the 'Episodes' section and highlight the Main Menu selection. Press RIGHT and a dot will appear to the left. Press ENTER to listen to the French Woman's distress call.

Lost Season One   Alternate Opening Credits:

From Main Menu, hit UP or DOWN until "Tales From the Island" is highlighted. Press LEFT and a cursor will go next to 'Disc 7'. Hit ENTER to see an alternative opening credits sequence.

Lost Season One   Alternate Version of The Climb:

On Disc #7 in the 'Bonus Feature' section choose deleted scenes. Now, choose 'The Climb" and press your SELECT or PLAY button. Then press your LEFT button three times. The first two will get no response but on the third a dot will appear on the screen, lit up as a selection. Press your ENTER button and you will see a hilarious alternate version of the end sequence of "The Climb."

Locke's Orange:

On Disc 7 (the Bonus Disc), access the 'Tales From the Island' option. Once in there, press RIGHT until the lock get's highlighted. Press ENTER to reveal a sequence of takes with Locke smiling with the orange in his mouth.

On The Web

Some Fun Sites

http://www.dharmaindustries.com
http://www.mrclucks.com
http://www.dharmainitiative.com/
http://www.dharmainitiative.org
http://www.dharmainitiative.info
http://www.dharmainitiative.net
http://www.DriveShaftband.com
http://www.thehansofoundation.com/

http://www.thehansofoundation.net/
http://www.oceanicfligh815.net
http://www.thedharmainitiative.org
http://www.hansofoundation.net/
http://www.hansofoundation.info/
http://www.hansofoundation.com/
http://www.hansofoundation.org/
http://www.bigspaceship1.com
http://www.oceanicworldair.com
http://marvincandle.com/
http://www.lostflight.com/
http://lostpedia.com/wiki/Main_Page

Official Sites
http://www.thehansofoundation.org/
http://www.oceanicflight815.com/
http://www.oceanic air.com/
http://www.fly oceanic.com
http://www.oceanic airlines.com
http://www.thefuselage.com

Fan Sites
Black Rock
http://www.blackrock.nl/component/option,com_simplebo
ard/Itemid,47/
Dharma Secrets
http://www.dharmasecrets.com
DM Ville
http://www.dmville.com/
Execute
http://soulykeeper.proboards25.com/index.cgi
FandomTalk
http://www.fandomtalk.com/forum/viewforum.php?f=22
Flight 815

http://www.flight815.info/
Get Lost
http://getlost.lschosting.info/
I Am Lost
http://s9.invisionfree.com/Iamlost
Jater Paradise
http://s14.invisionfree.com/Jaterparadise
Little Bit Losted
http://littlebitlosted.proboards34.com/index.cgi
Live Journal
http://www.livejournal.com/interests.bml?int=lost
Long Lost List
http://longlostlist.kazorum.com/
Looking Lost
http://lostforum.org/
Lost
http://www.aimoo.com/forum/freeboard.cfm?id=675212
http://www.lost.image22.net/
Lost 4 Ever
http://lost4everforums.proboards21.com/index.cgi
Lost Chat
http://www.lost chat.com/
Lost Community
http://www.lostcommunity.com/
Lost Discussion
http://lostdiscussion.com/
Lost Fanatic
http://lostfanatic.proboards43.com/
Lost Fanatics
http://lostfanatics.forumup.org/
Lost Fan Blog
http://s3.invisionfree.com/The_Fan_Blog_Forumn/
Lost Fan Forum
http://www.lostfanforum.com/lforum/
Lost FAQ
http://www.lostfaq.com
Lost Fans

http://lostfans.6te.net/modules.php?name=Forums
Lost Fever
http://www.lostfever.com/forums/
Lost Forum
http://lost forum.com/
Lost Horizons
http://p205.ezboard.com/bconversationswithdeadpeople
Lost Guild
http://losttvguild.11.forumer.com/index.php
Lost Investigations
http://www.lostinvestigations.com/discussions/
Lostits
http://lostits.proboards37.com/index.cgi
Lost Message Boards
http://lostmessageboards.short designs.com/
LostNReality
http://s11.invisionfree.com/LostNReality/index.php?http://
s11.invisionfree.com/LostNReality/
Lost Oceanic Flight 815
http://www.lostoceanicflight815.com/phpBB2/
Lost Panic
http://lostpanic.hosted forum.com/
Lost Podcast
http://lostpodcast.proboards2.com/index.cgi
Lost Rocks
http://lostrocksforum.forumup.org/
Lost Season 2
http://www.lostseason2.com/component/option,com_simpl
eboard/Itemid,29/
Lost Studies
http://loststudies.com/
Lost Talk
http://www.losttalk.info/boards/
http://www.losttalk.net/
Lost TV
http://www.losttv forum.com/forum/
Lostv Forums

http://www.lostv forums.com/

Lost Without A Map

http://lostwithoutamap.proboards50.com/

Oceanic Lost

http://www.oceaniclost.com/

Oceanic Theory

http://forums.go.com/abc/oceanic/index

SF Fandom

http://www.sf
fandom.com/vbulletin/forumdisplay.php?s=&daysprune=6
0&forumid=63

The Castaways

http://www.the castaways.net/

The Hatch Online

http://www.forums.thehatchonline.com/

The Lost Forum

http://s15.invisionfree.com/The_Lost_Forum/

The Losties

http://www.thelosties.com/forum/

The Tail Section

http://www.thetailsection.com/forums/

Television Without Pity

http://forums.televisionwithoutpity.com/index.php?s=0de8
9eea3794552c4d5db5f237a28641&showforum=707

TV Lost

http://www.tvlost.com/forum/

48 Survivors

http://www.48survivors.com/forum/

4815162342

http://www.4815162342.com/forum/

Debunked Theories

Season One Emmy Awards

   1. Outstanding Drama Series

2. Outstanding Directing for a Drama Series
3. Outstanding Cast for a Drama Series
4. Outstanding Single Camera Picture Editing for a Drama Series
5. Outstanding Music Composition for a Series
6. Outstanding Special Visual Effects for a Series

Season Two Episodes

Episode 2:1 Man of Science, Man of Faith
Episode 2:2 Adrift
Episode 2:3 Orientation
Episode 2:4 Everybody Hates Hugo
Episode 2:5...And Found
Episode 2:6 Abandoned
Episode 2:7 The Other 48 Days
Episode 2:8 Collision
Episode 2:9 What Kate Did
Episode 2:10 The 23rd Psalm
Episode 2:11 The Hunting Party
Episode 2:12 Fire + Water
Episode 2:13 The Long Con
Episode 2:14 One of Them

Printed in the United States
51438LVS00003B/71